Contemporary Psychometrics - New Developments and Applications

Edited by María Cristina Richaud, Belen Mesurado and Viviana Noemí Lemos

Published in London, United Kingdom

Contemporary Psychometrics - New Developments and Applications
http://dx.doi.org/10.5772/intechopen.1006787
Edited by María Cristina Richaud, Belen Mesurado and Viviana Noemí Lemos

Contributors
Anila Sadaf Mubashir, Deniz S. Ones, Kenneth J. Reid, Marcoantonio Villanueva Bustamante, Marei Ahmed, María Inés Acuña, Mirta Susana Ison, Rida Kainaat, Rolando Diaz-Loving, Silvina Alejandra Brussino, Sofia Rivera Aragon, Yilei Wang, Zekai Wei

First published in London, United Kingdom, 2025 by IntechOpen
IntechOpen is the global imprint of INTECHOPEN LIMITED, registered in England and Wales, registration number: 11086078, 167-169 Great Portland Street, London, W1W 5PF, United Kingdom

For EU product safety concerns: IN TECH d.o.o., Prolaz Marije Krucifikse Kozulić 3, 51000 Rijeka, Croatia, info@intechopen.com or visit our website at intechopen.com.

British Library Cataloguing-in-Publication Data
A catalogue record for this book is available from the British Library

Contemporary Psychometrics - New Developments and Applications
Edited by María Cristina Richaud, Belen Mesurado and Viviana Noemí Lemos
p. cm.
Print ISBN 978-1-83634-884-9
Online ISBN 978-1-83634-883-2
eBook (PDF) ISBN 978-1-83634-885-6

Meet the editors

María Cristina Richaud has a Ph.D. in Psychology from the University of Buenos Aires. She headed the Interdisciplinary Center of Research in Mathematical and Experimental Psychology (CIIPME), which is affiliated with the National Council of Scientific and Technical Research (CONICET) of Argentina, and has achieved the category of Superior Researcher of CONICET. Dr. Richaud currently works at the Institute of Family Sciences of the Universidad Austral and is a scientific advisor to the Universidad Adventista del Plata. Dr. Richaud's primary scholarly interests are in social cognitive variables in children and adolescents, parenting, and the study of problems faced by children at risk for poverty. For her distinguished work, she has received different awards, as the 2013 APA Award for Distinguished Contributions to the International Advancement of Psychology.

Viviana Lemos has a Ph.D. in Psychology from the National University of San Luis, Argentina. She is a Researcher at the National Council for Scientific and Technical Research (CONICET) in the Principal Researcher category. She currently directs the Interdisciplinary Center for Research in Health and Behavioral Sciences (CIICSAC) at the Universidad Adventista del Plata (UAP). She has made significant contributions to the training of human resources and authored more than a hundred scientific publications related to her research lines, focusing on the study, evaluation, and promotion of various socio-emotional resources in children and adolescents.

Belén Mesurado is a member of the Philosophy Institute and a Professor at Universidad Austral. She is a Principal Researcher at the National Scientific and Technical Research Council (CONICET). She obtained her undergraduate degree in Psychology (2003) and her Ph.D. in Psychology (2010) from Universidad Nacional de San Luis in Argentina. Her area of interest is Positive Psychology and prosocial behavior. She has received National Doctoral and Postdoctoral Scholarships from CONICET, as well as scholarships from prestigious international organizations such as Fundación Carolina, the Society for Research on Adolescence, the Society for Research in Child Development, and the International Union of Psychological Science. She has published 70 articles and 28 book chapters on various topics in Positive Psychology, has authored a book, and has presented more than 90 papers at national and international conferences.

Contents

Preface

Contemporary Psychometrics – New Developments and Applications brings together a diverse collection of chapters that reflect the dynamic and evolving landscape of psychometric research and applications. Aimed at specialists, scholars, and researchers in psychology, education, and related disciplines, this volume highlights both theoretical innovations and practical implementations that are reshaping how we understand and measure psychological constructs across cultures, contexts, and populations.

The book opens with *Transforming Psychometrics: Integrating Technology, and Application in the 21st Century* by Rida Kainaat and Anila Sadaf, offering a broad yet insightful overview of the field's recent progress. This chapter lays the foundation for subsequent discussions by outlining emerging methodological and conceptual frameworks.

María Inés Acuña and Silvina Alejandra Brussino contribute a compelling chapter on *Psychometric Network Analysis: An Alternative Approach to Understanding Psychosocial Systems*, presenting this alternative approach as a powerful lens for examining complex psychosocial systems. This perspective extends beyond traditional latent variable models and opens up new avenues for modeling interconnected psychological phenomena.

In *Ethnopsychometry: The Road to Valid, Reliable Yet Culturally Sensitive and Relevant Measures*, Rolando Díaz-Loving, Sofía Rivera Aragón, and Marco Antonio Villanueva Bustamante critically address the imperative of cultural relevance in psychometric tools. Their work challenges us to refine our methodologies to better serve diverse populations, emphasizing equity in psychological assessment.

The final section features empirical studies showcasing novel test development and validation efforts. Marei Ahmed, in the chapter *Reviewing the Translated and Validated Scales in Positive Psychology in Sports within Arabic-Speaking Countries*, provides valuable insights into cross-cultural adaptation and validation. Kenneth J. Reid's study, *Psychometric Analysis of an Instrument to Study Retention in Engineering: Do Results Support the Gender Similarity Hypothesis?*, examines gender similarities and contributes to ongoing conversations on inclusivity in STEM education. Lastly, Mirta Susana Ison introduces a *Computerized Child Attention Test*, illustrating the integration of technology and psychometric innovation in cognitive assessment.

Together, these contributions exemplify the rich variety of contemporary psychometric inquiry. We hope this volume will stimulate further research, foster interdisciplinary dialogue, and inspire new applications in both academic and applied settings.

María Cristina Richaud
National Council of Scientific and Technical Research (CONICET),
Buenos Aires, Argentina

Austral University,
Institute of Family Sciences,
Pilar, Argentina

Belen Mesurado,
Austral University,
Pilar, Argentina

Viviana Noemí Lemos
National Council of Scientific and Technical Research (CONICET),
Buenos Aires, Argentina

Section 1

Theoretical Approaches

Chapter 1

Transforming Psychometrics: Integrating Technology, and Application in the 21st Century

Anila Sadaf Mubashir and Rida Kainaat

Abstract

This chapter explores contemporary developments in psychometrics, emphasizing advanced models and methodologies that enhance the precision and applicability of psychological measurement. It traces the evolution from Classical Test Theory (CTT) to sophisticated frameworks like Item Response Theory (IRT), Bayesian psychometrics, and network psychometrics. These advancements enable personalized assessments, adaptive testing, and real-time updates, significantly improving educational, clinical, and organizational applications. The chapter also discusses ethical challenges, including data privacy, fairness, and interpretability, highlighting the need for transparent and unbiased assessments. With the integration of artificial intelligence (AI), big data analytics, and wearable technology, psychometrics is poised to revolutionize psychological measurement. The chapter concludes by emphasizing the importance of ethical considerations and cultural sensitivity in global applications, ensuring accurate and equitable psychological assessments.

Keywords: contemporary psychometrics, Item Response Theory (IRT), Bayesian psychometrics, adaptive testing, ethical considerations

1. Introduction

1.1 Historical context and traditional psychometric approaches

Psychometrics, the scientific discipline concerned with the measurement of psychological attributes such as intelligence, personality, and abilities, has its origins in the late nineteenth and early twentieth centuries. Early pioneers, including Francis Galton [1], Charles Spearman [2], and Alfred Binet [3], laid the foundation for the field by developing statistical techniques for measuring individual differences.

The first widely recognized psychometric models emerged in educational and psychological testing, with Classical Test Theory (CTT) being the dominant framework for test development and validation [4]. CTT is based on the assumption that an observed test score consists of a true score and an error component. Reliability and validity were key concerns, with early psychometricians devising methods to ensure consistency and accuracy in measurement [5].

Traditional psychometric assessments relied on summative scoring, where test-takers were evaluated based on aggregate scores without consideration of item-level variability [6]. This approach, while useful, had limitations, including an inability to account for differences in item difficulty and discrimination [7]. As the field progressed, researchers sought more refined models that could provide deeper insights into test performance and latent psychological constructs [8].

The shift from Classical Test Theory (CTT) to more sophisticated models while CTT provided foundational principles for psychometric assessments, it had several limitations. One of the major drawbacks was its dependence on sample-specific statistics, meaning that test properties could vary across different populations [9]. Additionally, CTT assumed that all test items contributed equally to the measurement of an underlying trait, which was an oversimplification of real-world psychological constructs [10].

To address these limitations, psychometricians developed Item Response Theory (IRT), a paradigm that models the probability of a test-taker responding correctly to an item based on their latent ability level [11]. Unlike CTT, IRT provides item-level information, allowing for more precise measurement and adaptive testing [8]. This shift marked a significant advancement in psychometrics, enabling the development of Computerized Adaptive Testing (CAT) [12], where test difficulty adjusts dynamically to an individual's performance.

Other sophisticated models, such as Bayesian psychometrics [13] and network psychometrics [14], have further expanded the scope of psychological measurement. Bayesian methods allow for real-time updating of ability estimates, improving the accuracy of adaptive learning systems [15]. Network psychometrics, in contrast, conceptualizes psychological traits as dynamic systems rather than single underlying constructs, offering new perspectives on mental health assessments and personality research [16].

1.2 Overview of the demand for advanced psychometrics in an increasingly data-driven world

The integration of big data and artificial intelligence (AI) has significantly reshaped the field of psychometrics. Traditional paper-based assessments have transitioned into digital and AI-driven methodologies, leading to a heightened demand for advanced psychometric models across various sectors, including education, healthcare, human resources, and AI applications.

In the educational domain, adaptive learning platforms utilize psychometric models to customize instruction, ensuring that students receive content tailored to their individual strengths and weaknesses. For instance, AI-based virtual tutor systems have been conceptualized to support students with learning difficulties by incorporating psychometric assessments to monitor and analyze behaviors, activities, and health-related patterns [17].

In clinical psychology, digital mental health tools employ psychometric assessments to monitor symptoms, forecast treatment outcomes, and deliver data-driven interventions. A notable example is MoodPath, an AI-driven application that assists users in tracking their mental health by evaluating their responses to questions about mood and daily activities [18].

Within organizational environments, psychometrics plays a crucial role in recruitment and employee evaluations. AI-enhanced psychometric assessments are revolutionizing talent evaluation by offering speed, scalability, and data-driven insights, thereby transforming the hiring landscape [19].

Moreover, AI and machine learning researchers apply psychometric principles to refine human-computer interactions, thereby improving user experiences on digital platforms. This involves integrating AI methodologies with psychological measurements to enhance the accuracy and efficiency of assessments.

The growing dependence on data-driven decision-making introduces new challenges for psychometricians, particularly concerning ethical issues related to data privacy, bias, and interpretability. Ensuring fairness and transparency in psychometric applications is paramount. For example, AI-driven psychometric assessments must address ethical challenges and data privacy concerns to maintain trust and uphold ethical standards.

As the field progresses, advancements in AI, wearable technology, and big data analytics are poised to further transform psychometrics, enhancing the precision, efficiency, and applicability of psychological measurements. Continuous validation and testing are essential to maintain the reliability of AI-powered psychometric assessments, ensuring they meet the evolving needs of various sectors.

2. Advancements in psychometric models and methodologies

2.1 Item Response Theory (IRT) and beyond: Exploring models for different types of data

Item Response Theory (IRT) has long served as a foundational framework in psychometrics, modeling test items based on parameters such as difficulty, discrimination, and guessing. Recent advancements have extended traditional IRT models to better accommodate complex data structures and provide more nuanced assessments.

2.1.1 Multidimensional Item Response Theory (MIRT)

Traditional IRT models often assume one-dimensionality, meaning they assess a single latent trait. However, many psychological and educational constructs are inherently multidimensional. MIRT addresses this by allowing for the simultaneous assessment of multiple latent traits, providing a more comprehensive understanding of test performance.

Recent developments in MIRT include

- *Sparse Bayesian MIRT:* [20] Li introduced a scalable Bayesian Expectation-Maximization algorithm designed to estimate sparse factor loadings from mixed continuous, binary, and ordinal item responses. This approach enhances interpretability and scalability, addressing challenges in high-dimensional data contexts.

- *Person explanatory MIRT:* This model integrates person-specific covariates into the MIRT framework, allowing for a more personalized assessment by considering individual differences beyond latent traits. Such integration facilitates tailored interventions and more accurate diagnostics.

2.1.2 Cognitive Diagnostic Models (CDMs)

CDMs aim to provide detailed information about individuals' specific strengths and weaknesses across various skills or attributes, enabling personalized feedback in educational and psychological assessments.

Recent advancements in CDMs include

- *Deep learning-based CDMs:* Wang et al. conducted a comprehensive survey highlighting the integration of deep learning techniques into CDMs. This fusion enhances the models' ability to capture complex, nonlinear relationships in data, leading to more accurate diagnostics and personalized interventions [21].

- *Deep Cognitive Diagnostic Models (DeepCDMs):* Chen et al. proposed a new family of DeepCDMs that leverage deep generative modeling to uncover deep discrete diagnostic information. These models offer advantages in identifiability, parsimony, and interpretability, making them valuable tools for detailed cognitive assessments.

- *ReliCD framework:* Zhang et al. developed the ReliCD framework, which incorporates confidence awareness into cognitive diagnosis. By quantifying the uncertainty in diagnostic feedback, this framework enhances the reliability of assessments, providing more trustworthy information for educational and psychological interventions [22].

2.2 Computerized Adaptive Testing (CAT): Tailoring assessments to individual test-takers

Computerized Adaptive Testing (CAT) utilizes Item Response Theory (IRT) to dynamically adjust the difficulty of test items based on a test-taker's responses, thereby enhancing assessment efficiency and precision. Recent advancements in CAT have focused on integrating Multistage Testing (MST) frameworks and leveraging artificial intelligence (AI) to further tailor assessments to individual test-takers.

2.2.1 Multistage testing (MST)

MST is an adaptive testing approach that administers assessments in multiple stages, with each stage comprising a set of items (modules) selected based on the test-taker's performance in previous stages. This structured approach allows for a balance between the adaptability of CAT and the practical constraints of test administration. Recent developments have seen the integration of MST with CAT methodologies, resulting in hybrid models that combine the item-level adaptability of CAT with the structured modular approach of MST. Such hybrid models aim to optimize test efficiency and measurement precision. For instance, research has demonstrated that combining CAT and MST can effectively enhance the adaptability and accuracy of assessments [23].

2.2.2 AI-driven adaptive assessments

The incorporation of AI into CAT has led to significant improvements in the adaptability and personalization of assessments. Machine learning algorithms can analyze extensive datasets of test-taker responses to predict ability levels more accurately and select items that are optimally informative. This AI-driven approach enables real-time adjustments to the assessment process, ensuring that each test-taker receives a unique set of items tailored to their ability level. Moreover, AI facilitates the continuous generation of new test items that maintain psychometric properties, thereby reducing the risk of item exposure and enhancing test security. For example, AI techniques have been employed to create sophisticated algorithms that improve the precision and efficiency of adaptive testing systems [24]. Recent studies have explored various facets of CAT, MST, and AI integration. A comprehensive survey by Liu et al. [24] discusses the application of machine learning techniques in CAT, highlighting how these methods can optimize item selection algorithms and improve the overall testing experience. Additionally, research has focused on balancing test accuracy and security in CAT by employing AI-driven methods to control item exposure and maintain the integrity of the assessment process [25]. Furthermore, advancements in multidimensional CAT have been proposed, utilizing multidimensional Item Response Theory to assess multiple latent traits simultaneously, thereby providing a more holistic evaluation of test-takers' abilities [26].

2.3 Bayesian psychometrics: Applications in adaptive learning and personalized assessments

Bayesian psychometrics has emerged as a powerful framework for enhancing adaptive learning and personalized assessments by incorporating probabilistic reasoning into psychometric modeling. Unlike traditional approaches that rely on static estimates of ability, Bayesian methods continuously update a learner's proficiency based on new evidence, refining predictions in real-time. Bayesian networks facilitate dynamic decision-making by modeling dependencies among multiple cognitive skills, allowing for a more granular assessment of strengths and weaknesses. Hierarchical Bayesian models further enhance this adaptability by accounting for variations at multiple levels, such as individual differences, group-level learning patterns, and item-level characteristics. These advancements have significantly improved adaptive learning systems by enabling more precise, data-driven instructional strategies. For instance, AI-powered tutoring systems leverage Bayesian inference to predict knowledge retention, optimize question sequencing, and provide timely interventions tailored to each learner's needs. Additionally, Bayesian adaptive assessments enhance test efficiency by selecting items that maximize information gain while minimizing test length, ensuring both accuracy and engagement. As educational technology continues to evolve, integrating Bayesian psychometrics with machine learning and big data analytics will further personalize education, making assessments more responsive, equitable, and effective in fostering long-term learning outcomes.

2.4 Network psychometrics: Conceptualizing psychological constructs as networks

Network psychometrics represents a paradigm shift in psychological measurement by conceptualizing psychological constructs as dynamic networks of interconnected variables rather than as manifestations of latent traits. Unlike traditional psychometric models that assume a unidirectional relationship between latent traits and observed responses, network psychometrics views psychological attributes as emergent properties of interacting components. This perspective is particularly valuable in mental health assessments, where symptoms are often interdependent rather than stemming from a single underlying disorder. For example, in depression, symptoms like insomnia, fatigue, and lack of motivation may reinforce each other, creating feedback loops that sustain the disorder. By mapping these interactions, network models provide insights into symptom structures, helping clinicians identify key symptoms that drive distress and may serve as intervention targets. Furthermore, recent advancements in computational methods, such as graphical LASSO and Bayesian network modeling, have enhanced the precision and applicability of network psychometrics across various psychological domains. This approach also aligns with person-centered and idiographic methodologies, allowing for individualized assessments that adapt to the unique symptom networks of each person. As psychological science embraces complexity, network psychometrics offers a robust framework for understanding mental health, personality traits, and cognitive abilities in ways that traditional models cannot fully capture.

3. Applications of modern psychometrics

Psychometrics, the scientific study of psychological measurement, has significantly evolved with modern technology. With the advancement of data analytics, artificial intelligence (AI), and sophisticated statistical models, psychometrics is now widely applied across various fields. This note explores its applications in education, clinical psychology, organizational settings, and AI/machine learning (**Table 1**).

3.1 Applications in education

Modern psychometrics has revolutionized the education sector by enabling personalized learning experiences and improving skill assessment methods. Key applications include.

3.1.1 Personalized learning platforms

Psychometric tools help tailor educational content according to students' cognitive abilities, learning styles, and preferences. Platforms such as adaptive learning management systems (LMS) utilize psychometric data to recommend learning pathways, ensuring that students receive content at an appropriate difficulty level. For example, imagine a middle school student using an adaptive learning platform like DreamBox. These platforms analyze the student's past performance on math problems and tailor

Field	Key applications	Description
Education	Personalized learning platforms, skill assessment, and adaptive testing.	Tailors educational content to students' needs and provides dynamic assessments for accurate skill measurement.
Clinical psychology	Psychological diagnostics, mental health screening, and outcome prediction.	Diagnoses mental health conditions, screens at-risk individuals, and predicts treatment effectiveness.
Organizational setting	Recruitment and selection, employee assessment, and performance monitoring.	Enhances hiring processes, evaluates employee competencies, and tracks performance metrics.
AI and machine learning	Human-computer interaction, user profiling, and behavioral prediction.	Improves user experience, personalizes content, and predicts human behavior using psychometric data.

Table 1.
Applications of modern psychometrics.

the difficulty of future questions accordingly. If the student struggles with fractions, the system provides additional practice problems and explanatory videos. Conversely, if the student excels in algebra, it accelerates their learning path by introducing more advanced topics, ensuring an individualized learning experience.

3.1.2 Skill assessment

Standardized testing has evolved with psychometric advancements to measure a student's abilities more accurately. Instead of static assessments, modern systems employ Item Response Theory (IRT) to dynamically adjust question difficulty based on student responses, providing a more precise evaluation of knowledge and skills. For example, the Duolingo English Test (DET) is a modern language proficiency exam that adapts to a test-taker's skill level using psychometric principles. Instead of presenting a fixed set of questions, the test dynamically adjusts question difficulty based on responses, ensuring a more precise measurement of language abilities. This contrasts with traditional standardized exams like the TOEFL or IELTS, which use a static question format and may not fully capture the range of a test-taker's proficiency.

3.1.3 Adaptive testing

Computerized Adaptive Testing (CAT) leverages psychometric models to personalize test difficulty in real-time. This enhances both efficiency and accuracy in measuring student proficiency, reducing test-taking time while maintaining reliability. For example, the Graduate Management Admission Test (GMAT) uses Computerized Adaptive Testing (CAT) to assess candidates' quantitative and verbal reasoning abilities. When a test-taker answers a question correctly, the next question becomes more difficult. If they answer incorrectly, the system presents an easier question. This method allows the GMAT to evaluate proficiency efficiently, requiring fewer questions while maintaining accuracy in score estimation. It also minimizes test anxiety by ensuring that each examinee faces questions that match their ability level.

3.2 Applications in clinical psychology

Psychometrics is extensively used in clinical psychology for diagnosing mental health conditions, screening patients, and predicting treatment outcomes.

3.2.1 Psychological diagnostics

Clinicians use psychometric assessments, such as the Minnesota Multiphasic Personality Inventory (MMPI) and Beck Depression Inventory (BDI), to diagnose mental health disorders. These tests are designed to identify patterns of behavior and cognitive functioning that align with psychological conditions. For example, a psychologist evaluating a patient for depression may administer the Beck Depression Inventory (BDI-II) to assess the severity of depressive symptoms. The patient's responses help determine whether they meet the clinical criteria for major depressive disorder. Similarly, a clinician diagnosing personality disorders might use the Minnesota Multiphasic Personality Inventory (MMPI-2-RF), which provides a detailed psychological profile based on scales measuring traits such as paranoia, anxiety, and social introversion.

3.2.2 Mental health screening

Online and digital psychometric tools enable large-scale mental health screenings. AI-driven questionnaires and self-report inventories assist healthcare providers in identifying individuals at risk for conditions like depression, anxiety, or PTSD, allowing for early intervention. For example, a university counseling center implements an AI-driven mental health screening tool that students can access online. The tool utilizes a combination of self-report questions and machine learning algorithms to detect early signs of anxiety and depression. If a student's responses indicate moderate to severe distress, the system automatically refers them to a counselor for further evaluation. This approach allows for large-scale early detection and intervention.

3.2.3 Outcome prediction

Predictive analytics in psychometrics helps gauge the effectiveness of treatments based on patient responses to psychological tests. By analyzing historical patient data, clinicians can anticipate treatment success rates and adjust therapeutic strategies accordingly. For example, a psychiatrist treating patients with generalized anxiety disorder uses predictive analytics to determine which treatment plan is most likely to be effective. By analyzing data from previous patients who have taken the Generalized Anxiety Disorder-7 (GAD-7) scale, the system predicts whether a particular patient will respond better to cognitive-behavioral therapy (CBT) or medication. Based on these insights, the psychiatrist tailors the treatment plan to improve the likelihood of success.

3.3 Applications in organizational settings

Businesses and organizations employ psychometric techniques for workforce management, ensuring optimal hiring decisions and performance tracking.

3.3.1 Recruitment and selection

Companies utilize psychometric assessments such as aptitude tests, personality inventories, and cognitive ability tests to predict candidate job performance. These tests help organizations make data-driven hiring decisions, improving workforce quality. For example, a multinational tech company like Google utilizes psychometric assessments to streamline its hiring process. Candidates applying for software engineering roles undergo cognitive ability tests assessing problem-solving skills, logical reasoning, and numerical aptitude. Additionally, personality inventories like the Big Five model help identify traits such as conscientiousness and openness, ensuring cultural fit and predicting long-term job performance. By leveraging psychometric techniques, Google minimizes hiring biases and selects candidates who align best with the company's values and job requirements.

3.3.2 Employee assessment

Modern psychometrics aids in evaluating employee competencies, strengths, and areas requiring development. Many firms incorporate psychometric evaluations in annual performance reviews to enhance productivity and align employee skills with job roles. For example, a financial services firm like JP integrates psychometric evaluations into its annual performance reviews. Employees take skills-based tests measuring their analytical reasoning, leadership potential, and adaptability to fast-changing financial markets. Additionally, emotional intelligence (EQ) assessments help managers understand an employee's interpersonal strengths and areas needing improvement. By using these insights, the company tailors professional development plans, offering targeted training programs to enhance employee competencies.

3.3.3 Performance monitoring

Continuous psychometric tracking allows organizations to assess employee engagement, motivation, and job satisfaction. Tools like 360-degree feedback assessments help in identifying areas where interventions are needed to maintain a healthy work environment. For example, a global retail giant like Amazon employs continuous psychometric tracking to measure employee engagement and job satisfaction. Tools such as Gallup's Q12 engagement survey and 360-degree feedback mechanisms collect insights from peers, subordinates, and managers, identifying strengths and performance gaps. If the data reveals declining motivation in warehouse employees, targeted interventions—such as workload restructuring or wellness programs—are introduced to improve morale and productivity. This approach fosters a proactive work culture, ensuring employee well-being and sustained high performance.

3.4 Applications in AI and machine learning

With the rise of AI, psychometrics has become an essential tool in human-computer interaction, user profiling, and behavioral analytics.

3.4.1 Human-computer interaction

AI-driven psychometric assessments improve user experience by analyzing cognitive patterns and preferences. AI systems adapt interfaces and functionalities to user behavior, enhancing usability and engagement. For example, adaptive learning platforms: AI-driven psychometric assessments are widely used in adaptive learning systems like Duolingo and Coursera. These platforms analyze users' cognitive patterns, learning speed, and engagement levels to personalize lesson difficulty and content delivery. By understanding whether a learner struggles with a particular topic, the AI adapts the interface, provides tailored exercises, and suggests optimal learning paths, improving the overall user experience and retention.

3.4.2 User profiling

Psychometric models are integrated into AI systems to understand user traits, preferences, and behaviors. Social media platforms and e-commerce websites use these insights to personalize recommendations and advertisements. For example, streaming services like Netflix and Spotify leverage psychometric-based AI models to analyze user preferences, moods, and behavior. For instance, Spotify's recommendation engine assesses users' listening habits, frequency of song skips, and engagement with different genres to curate personalized playlists. Similarly, Netflix uses psychometric profiling to suggest content based on users' viewing history, personality-based engagement, and past interactions, leading to more relevant and engaging recommendations.

3.4.3 Behavioral prediction

AI utilizes psychometric data to predict human decision-making patterns. This is particularly beneficial in fields such as cybersecurity (for detecting potential threats) and finance (for risk assessment in investments and lending). For example, financial institutions like JP and PayPal use AI-powered psychometric models to detect fraudulent transactions and assess credit risk. By analyzing a user's spending behavior, transaction history, and digital footprint, AI predicts deviations from normal financial behavior, flagging potential fraud. Additionally, psychometric insights help assess a borrower's likelihood of loan repayment, factoring in behavioral patterns, social media activity, and even linguistic analysis of loan applications to make risk assessments more accurate.

4. Challenges in contemporary psychometrics

Psychometrics, the field of study concerned with the theory and technique of psychological measurement, has evolved significantly with advancements in data science and artificial intelligence. However, contemporary psychometrics faces numerous challenges that impact the validity, reliability, and ethical use of psychological assessments. Four major challenges in this field include data privacy and security, fairness and bias, interpretability, and ethical considerations. Each of these aspects presents unique obstacles and demands careful attention from researchers, practitioners, and policymakers.

4.1 Data privacy and security: Ensuring participant data remains protected

With the growing use of digital psychometric assessments, safeguarding participant data has become a critical challenge. Online assessments, cloud-based storage, and automated scoring systems have increased the risk of data breaches, unauthorized access, and misuse of sensitive information.

4.1.1 Risk of data breaches

The storage and transmission of psychometric data on digital platforms make it susceptible to cyberattacks. Hackers can exploit vulnerabilities to access personal and psychological profiles, leading to identity theft or manipulation. For example, in 2021, a major online mental health assessment platform experienced a data breach in which hackers accessed thousands of psychological evaluations. The breach exposed sensitive participant responses, including details about mental health conditions and personality traits. This incident raised concerns about the security of digital psychometric assessments and highlighted the need for stronger encryption measures and cybersecurity protocols.

4.1.2 Regulatory compliance

Psychometric assessments must adhere to data protection laws such as the General Data Protection Regulation (GDPR) in Europe and the Health Insurance Portability and Accountability Act (HIPAA) in the United States. Ensuring compliance with these regulations is complex, especially when assessments are administered globally. For example, a multinational company deploying a pre-employment psychometric test faced legal challenges when it failed to comply with GDPR. Since the test collected behavioral and cognitive data from applicants in the EU, the company was required to ensure explicit consent, data portability, and the right to erasure. However, due to a lack of compliance mechanisms, the company was fined and had to redesign its assessment process to align with data protection regulations.

4.1.3 Anonymization and encryption

To protect participant identities, psychometric data should be anonymized and encrypted. However, achieving a balance between data utility and privacy remains a challenge. For example, a university conducting large-scale psychological research implemented advanced encryption protocols to protect participant data. Before storing responses in a cloud-based system, the researchers removed personally identifiable information and replaced it with anonymized codes. However, the challenge arose when some researchers needed identifiable data for follow-up studies, forcing them to establish a secure re-identification process while maintaining privacy safeguards.

4.1.4 Informed consent

Many test-takers are unaware of how their data will be used. Transparent communication about data collection, storage, and sharing practices is essential to maintaining trust and ethical integrity. For example, a popular mobile app offering personality assessments was criticized when users discovered their data was being sold to third-party companies for targeted advertising. Although the app included a terms-of-service agreement, it was lengthy and complex, leading many users to consent without fully understanding the implications. Following public backlash, the company revised its consent process by introducing a simplified, transparent disclosure explaining how data would be stored, used, and shared.

4.2 Fairness and bias: Addressing disparities in test outcomes across demographics

Bias in psychometric assessments can result in unfair disadvantages for certain demographic groups, leading to discrimination in educational, employment, and clinical settings.

4.2.1 Cultural and linguistic bias

Many standardized tests are designed for specific cultural and linguistic groups, leading to disparities in performance for individuals from different backgrounds. For example, a widely used intelligence test includes verbal reasoning items that require familiarity with idiomatic English expressions. Test-takers who are non-native English speakers or come from culturally diverse backgrounds may struggle with these questions, not because of cognitive limitations but due to differences in linguistic exposure. As a result, their scores may be lower, leading to misinterpretations of their intellectual abilities and unfair disadvantages in educational placements.

4.2.2 Algorithmic bias

As machine learning models are increasingly used for test scoring and interpretation, biases embedded in training data can lead to skewed outcomes that disadvantage minority groups. For example, a company implements an AI-driven hiring assessment that predicts job performance based on past successful applicants. If historical hiring data disproportionately favors one demographic group (e.g., men over women), the algorithm may learn to prioritize candidates from that group, unintentionally discriminating against equally qualified female candidates. This bias can perpetuate systemic inequalities in hiring, even if the company did not intend to discriminate.

4.2.3 Socioeconomic disparities

Test-takers from lower socioeconomic backgrounds may have limited access to preparatory resources, resulting in lower scores that do not accurately reflect their true potential. For example, standardized college entrance exams often correlate with access to expensive test prep courses, tutoring, and high-quality schooling. A student from a low-income background, who lacks these resources, may score lower than a wealthier peer despite having similar intelligence and academic potential. This score disparity can limit their college opportunities, reinforcing social inequities rather than measuring true ability.

4.2.4 Mitigating bias

Strategies such as differential item functioning (DIF) analysis, diverse sample representation, and bias-aware algorithmic design can help reduce disparities and enhance fairness in assessments. For example, to address fairness in standardized testing, educational institutions implement differential item functioning (DIF) analysis, which examines whether test questions function differently for different demographic groups despite equal ability levels. Additionally, AI-based hiring assessments can be trained on diverse datasets and evaluated for bias before deployment. Universities and organizations also introduce income-based fee waivers and free test prep resources to level the playing field for test-takers from disadvantaged backgrounds.

4.3 Interpretability: Balancing complexity with transparency for end users

Advancements in psychometrics, particularly with AI-driven assessments, have led to increased complexity in test design and interpretation. However, ensuring that test results are understandable to both professionals and test-takers remains a significant challenge.

4.3.1 Black box models

Many modern psychometric tools use machine learning algorithms that provide highly accurate predictions but lack transparency, making it difficult for users to understand how decisions are made. For example, a company develops an AI-driven hiring assessment that predicts job performance based on psychometric test results and workplace behavior patterns. The algorithm uses deep learning, but hiring managers cannot understand why certain candidates are recommended over others. Without transparency, there is concern about potential bias and fairness in the selection process, leading to hesitation in fully trusting the tool.

4.3.2 User-friendly reporting

Test results should be presented in a clear and accessible manner for educators, employers, and clinicians. Complex statistical outputs should be translated into actionable insights. For example, a school implements a new computerized adaptive test for student learning assessments. Instead of providing raw statistical scores (e.g., factor loadings or percentile ranks), the results are presented in an easy-to-read dashboard. The report highlights strengths and areas for improvement using visual aids like progress bars and recommendations for personalized learning strategies, making the data actionable for teachers and students.

4.3.3 Trade-off between accuracy and simplicity

While advanced models improve precision, simpler models are often preferred for practical application. Finding a balance between sophistication and usability is a key challenge. For example, a mental health platform offers two depression screening tools: a simple 10-item self-report scale and a more sophisticated AI-driven adaptive test that adjusts questions based on previous answers. While the AI model provides highly precise assessments, many clinicians prefer the simpler tool because it is faster to administer and easier to explain to patients, demonstrating the challenge of balancing precision with practicality.

4.3.4 Training and education

End users, including HR professionals and clinicians, need proper training in interpreting psychometric data responsibly to avoid misinterpretation and misuse. For example, an HR department adopts a new psychometric assessment for employee leadership potential. Without adequate training, HR staff misinterpret the results, believing that lower scores indicate an employee's inability to lead rather than areas for development. To prevent misinterpretation, the company organizes workshops to teach HR professionals how to properly interpret test results and apply them in decision-making responsibly.

4.4 Ethical considerations: Implications for using psychometric assessments in sensitive contexts

The application of psychometric assessments in sensitive contexts, such as mental health diagnosis, employment screening, and legal settings, raises significant ethical concerns.

4.4.1 Informed consent and autonomy

Participants must have full knowledge of how their data will be used and retain the right to withdraw from assessments without consequences. For example, a university conducts a large-scale mental health survey among students to assess stress levels and psychological well-being. However, students later discovered that their responses were shared with faculty members without their explicit consent, leading to concerns about privacy and autonomy. Ethical guidelines emphasize that participants should be fully informed about data usage and have the right to opt out without facing academic or institutional consequences.

4.4.2 Misuse in employment and education

Organizations may use psychometric results to unfairly exclude candidates, leading to discrimination and ethical violations. For example, in 2017, a lawsuit was filed against a major corporation for using a personality test in hiring that disproportionately screened out candidates with certain mental health conditions. The test results were used to reject applicants who displayed traits associated with anxiety or depression, raising concerns about workplace discrimination. Similarly, some universities have been criticized for using cognitive ability tests in admissions in ways that reinforce socioeconomic disparities.

4.4.3 Psychological harm

Poorly designed assessments or misinterpretation of results can cause psychological distress to individuals, affecting their self-esteem and decision-making. For example, a school implements a high-stakes intelligence assessment to track students into gifted programs. A student who scores lower than expected experiences significant self-doubt and anxiety, leading to a decline in academic performance. Similarly, in clinical settings, individuals receiving inaccurate or overly rigid psychological test interpretations may develop negative self-perceptions, impacting their mental well-being and life choices.

4.4.4 Regulatory oversight

There is a need for clear ethical guidelines and oversight mechanisms to ensure the responsible use of psychometric assessments in various domains. For example, the use of psychometric assessments in forensic psychology has been scrutinized in legal cases where unreliable psychological tests influenced court decisions. For instance, the Minnesota Multiphasic Personality Inventory (MMPI) has been used in child custody disputes and parole hearings, sometimes without sufficient validation for those specific contexts. In response, organizations like the American Psychological Association (APA) and the Equal Employment Opportunity Commission (EEOC) have established guidelines to regulate the ethical use of these assessments, ensuring fairness and accountability.

5. Future directions in psychometrics

Psychometrics, the field of study focused on the theory and technique of psychological measurement, has evolved dramatically over the years. As technology continues to advance, the discipline is expanding into new areas, bringing innovative tools, approaches, and methodologies. The future of psychometrics is poised to incorporate cutting-edge technologies such as artificial intelligence (AI), wearable devices, and big data analytics, while also extending its reach globally through cross-cultural assessments. This chapter will explore several future directions in psychometrics, focusing on four key themes: the potential of AI in psychometric test development and analysis, integrating psychometrics with wearable technology and big data, predictive psychometrics for behavior prediction, and the opportunities for psychometrics in global and cross-cultural assessments.

5.1 Potential of AI in psychometric test development and analysis

Artificial intelligence (AI) has become a transformative force in many fields, and psychometrics is no exception. The integration of AI into psychometric test development and analysis presents exciting possibilities for improving the precision, accessibility, and efficiency of assessments.

5.1.1 AI-driven test development

AI has the potential to revolutionize the way psychometric tests are created. Traditional test development is a time-consuming process that requires careful item construction, validation, and pilot testing. AI can streamline this process by analyzing large datasets of test responses to identify patterns, trends, and correlations that would be difficult for human designers to detect. Machine learning algorithms can suggest test items that are likely to provide the most reliable and valid measures of a specific construct. Additionally, AI can optimize test item selection by ensuring that items are balanced across different subgroups of test-takers, enhancing fairness and inclusivity in assessments.

AI can also help in the process of Item Response Theory (IRT) modeling, which is widely used in psychometrics for assessing the relationship between test items and latent traits. By using AI-based methods, psychometricians can more easily model the complex, nonlinear relationships between item responses and latent traits, leading to more precise and individualized assessments.

5.1.2 Real-time data analysis and feedback

AI can be leveraged to provide real-time data analysis and feedback during the testing process. This means that psychometric tests can be continuously monitored for signs of bias, fatigue, or inconsistencies in response patterns, allowing for immediate adjustments to be made to ensure that the assessment remains valid and reliable throughout its administration. This capability can significantly enhance the testing experience, making it more adaptive and responsive to the needs of individual test-takers.

Moreover, AI-driven platforms can analyze patterns in responses to suggest areas for further exploration or development, thus improving the overall utility of psychometric tests. This data-driven approach could lead to the creation of more accurate, personalized, and predictive assessments of psychological traits.

5.2 Integrating psychometrics with wearable technology and big data

Wearable technology, such as fitness trackers, smartwatches, and biosensors, has become increasingly popular in recent years. These devices can provide continuous streams of physiological data, which can be invaluable for psychometricians seeking to understand the relationship between physical and psychological states. When integrated with psychometric assessments, wearable technology offers a new frontier for measuring psychological constructs.

5.2.1 Physiological data integration

Wearable devices capture a wide range of physiological data, including heart rate, skin conductance, sleep patterns, and physical activity. By integrating these physiological indicators with psychometric assessments, researchers and clinicians can gain deeper insights into how these physiological markers are related to psychological traits, such as stress, anxiety, or cognitive performance. For example, researchers could use data from a smartwatch to measure a person's stress levels during a test or their emotional responses to specific stimuli, providing an additional layer of information that complements traditional self-report measures.

This integration allows for a more holistic approach to psychological measurement, where psychometrics no longer relies solely on self-reported data or structured interviews but also incorporates real-time biological indicators. This can enhance the ecological validity of assessments by capturing data in naturalistic settings, outside of laboratory conditions.

5.2.2 Big data analytics

The advent of big data has opened up new opportunities for psychometrics. With the ability to collect and analyze vast amounts of data, psychometricians can examine large datasets from diverse populations, allowing for the identification of trends and patterns that may not have been apparent in smaller, more homogenous samples. Big data analytics enables the development of more robust models of psychological traits that are based on a wider range of data sources, including social media interactions, online behavior, and health data.

Through the use of machine learning and data mining techniques, psychometricians can uncover hidden relationships between psychological constructs and other variables, such as environmental factors, genetics, or life experiences. These insights could lead to more predictive and personalized psychometric models, offering the potential to assess not only psychological traits but also the ways in which these traits evolve over time.

5.2.3 Personalized psychometrics

The combination of wearable technology and big data can facilitate personalized psychometrics, where assessments are tailored to the individual. By continuously monitoring a person's physiological and behavioral responses over time, psychometric systems can dynamically adjust to provide assessments that are unique to each person's needs, context, and psychological state. Personalized assessments could help to provide more accurate and context-sensitive results, allowing clinicians and researchers to gain a deeper understanding of an individual's psychological functioning.

5.3 Predictive psychometrics: Leveraging psychometric models for behavior prediction

Predictive psychometrics involves the use of psychometric models to predict future behavior or outcomes based on an individual's psychological traits. This has significant implications for various fields, including education, healthcare, and organizational psychology.

DOI: http://dx.doi.org/10.5772/intechopen.1011724

5.3.1 Predicting academic and career success

One of the most promising applications of predictive psychometrics is in the prediction of academic and career success. Traditional psychometric tests, such as intelligence tests or personality assessments, have been used for decades to predict performance in specific domains. However, predictive psychometrics takes this a step further by integrating multiple data sources—such as past performance, behavioral patterns, and psychological traits—to predict future outcomes more accurately.

In education, predictive models could help identify students at risk of academic underperformance or those in need of additional support, allowing for early intervention and personalized learning strategies. Similarly, in the workplace, predictive psychometrics could be used to assess job candidates' likelihood of success in specific roles or predict how an individual's career trajectory may unfold based on their cognitive abilities, personality traits, and emotional intelligence.

5.3.2 Personalized interventions

Predictive psychometrics can also play a crucial role in the development of personalized interventions. By understanding the psychological traits and behaviors that predict certain outcomes, mental health professionals can tailor therapeutic interventions to the unique needs of each individual. For example, predictive models could help determine which types of therapy are most likely to be effective for a particular individual based on their personality traits and behavioral patterns.

5.3.3 Early detection of psychological disorders

Another potential application of predictive psychometrics is in the early detection of psychological disorders. Using predictive models based on data from psychometric tests and other sources, it may be possible to identify individuals who are at risk for developing mental health conditions, such as depression, anxiety, or substance abuse. Early detection could lead to timely interventions that could prevent or mitigate the onset of these disorders, improving overall mental health outcomes.

5.4 Opportunities for psychometrics in global and cross-cultural assessments

As psychometrics continues to expand globally, there is a growing need for assessments that are culturally sensitive and relevant across different regions and populations. Cross-cultural psychometrics offers an exciting opportunity to develop tools that can measure psychological traits and behaviors in diverse cultural contexts.

5.4.1 Cultural sensitivity in test design

One of the challenges in cross-cultural psychometrics is ensuring that tests are culturally appropriate and fair. Traditional psychometric assessments, which are often developed in Western contexts, may not always be suitable for use in non-Western cultures due to differences in language, values, and social norms. As a result, there is a need for more culturally sensitive test design that takes into account these differences while maintaining the validity and reliability of the assessment.

AI and machine learning can play a crucial role in this process by analyzing large, diverse datasets to identify culturally relevant items and response patterns. These technologies can help create assessments that are more inclusive and provide meaningful measures of psychological traits across different cultural contexts.

5.4.2 Global collaboration and data sharing

The future of psychometrics will likely involve increased collaboration across borders, with researchers and organizations from different countries working together to develop and validate psychometric assessments. Global collaborations can lead to the creation of more universally applicable tests, as well as the sharing of large, diverse datasets that can help improve the accuracy and generalizability of psychometric models.

Big data and AI can facilitate this global collaboration by enabling the collection and analysis of data from a variety of cultural contexts. This data can then be used to refine psychometric assessments, ensuring that they are applicable and meaningful for people from different cultural backgrounds.

5.4.3 Addressing global mental health issues

Psychometrics also holds promise for addressing global mental health issues. By developing culturally sensitive assessments, psychometric tools can help identify mental health challenges in diverse populations and provide valuable insights for designing targeted interventions. Global mental health initiatives can benefit from psychometric assessments that capture a wide range of psychological traits and behaviors, enabling more accurate diagnoses and effective treatments.

6. Conclusion

The field of psychometrics has undergone a significant transformation, evolving from traditional Classical Test Theory (CTT) to more sophisticated models such as Item Response Theory (IRT), Bayesian psychometrics, and network psychometrics. These advancements have enabled more precise measurement of psychological constructs and have expanded applications across diverse fields, including education, clinical psychology, organizational settings, and artificial intelligence. Modern psychometrics is increasingly driven by technological advancements, including AI, machine learning, and big data analytics. These innovations have improved the accuracy, efficiency, and adaptability of psychological assessments, making them more relevant in today's data-driven world. However, contemporary psychometrics also faces critical challenges, such as ensuring data privacy, reducing bias, maintaining interpretability, and addressing ethical concerns. Looking ahead, the integration of psychometrics with wearable technology, predictive analytics, and cross-cultural assessments offers promising opportunities for more personalized and globally applicable psychological measurements. The continued evolution of psychometric methodologies will be essential in addressing the growing demand for fair, accurate, and context-sensitive assessments in various domains.

Acknowledgements

The authors acknowledge the use of meta AI, for making of general chapter outline.

DOI: http://dx.doi.org/10.5772/intechopen.1011724

Conflict of interest

The authors declare no conflict of interest.

Author details

Anila Sadaf Mubashir and Rida Kainaat*
Department of Applied Psychology, National University of Modern Languages, Rawalpindi, Pakistan

*Address all correspondence to: rida.kainaat@numl.edu.pk

References

[1] Galton F. Hereditary Genius. London: Macmillan; 1869

[2] Spearman C. 'General intelligence,' objectively determined and measured. The American Journal of Psychology. 1904;**15**(2):201-293. DOI: 10.2307/1412107

[3] Binet and Simon. Méthodes nouvelles pour le diagnostic du niveau intellectuel des anormaux. L'Année Psychologique. 1905;**11**:191-336

[4] Lord FM, Novick MR. Statistical Theories of Mental Test Scores. Boston, Massachusetts, USA: Addison-Wesley; 1968

[5] Cronbach LJ. Coefficient alpha and the internal structure of tests. Psychometrika. 1951;**16**(3):297-334

[6] Thorndike EL. The nature, purposes, and general methods of measurements of educational products. Teachers College Record. 1918;**19**:1-20

[7] Gulliksen H. Theory of Mental Tests. New York: Wiley; 1950

[8] Embretson SE, Reise SP. Item Response Theory for Psychologists. Hove, East Sussex, UK: Psychology Press; 2000

[9] Hambleton RK, Swaminathan H. Item Response Theory: Principles and Applications. Boston, USA: Kluwer; 1985

[10] Messick S. Validity. In: Linn RL, editor. Educational Measurement. 3rd ed. New York, USA: Macmillan; 1989. pp. 13-103

[11] Rasch G. Probabilistic Models for some Intelligence and Attainment Tests. Copenhagen, Denmark: Danmarks Paedagogiske Institut; 1960

[12] Wainer H, Dorans NJ. Computerized Adaptive Testing: A Primer. New Jersey: Lawrence Erlbaum Associates; 2000

[13] Levy R. Bayesian Psychometric Modeling. UK: Cambridge University Press, Chapman and Hall/CRC; 2016

[14] Epskamp S, Fried EI. A tutorial on regularized partial correlation networks. Psychological Methods. 2018;**23**(4):617-634

[15] Van der Linden WJ. Handbook of Item Response Theory: Volume One. Roca Raton, New York: CRC Press; 2016

[16] Borsboom D. Psychometric perspectives on diagnostic systems. Psychological Medicine. 2008;**38**(10):1391-1401

[17] Hu A. Developing an AI based psychometric system for assessing learning difficulties and adaptive system to overcome: A qualitative and conceptual framework. arXiv preprint, arXiv:2403.06284. 2024. Published March 10, 2024

[18] Reed V. AI in psychological assessment. In: AI-BLOG: Where Tomorrow Begins Today. AI Proficiency Hub #aicompetence.org

[19] HRTech Staff Writer. Advancements in AI-Driven Psychometric Assessment Tools. In: TechRseries. TechRseries. Available from: https://techrseries.com/featured/advancements-in-ai-driven-psychometric-assessment-tools/

[20] Li Z, Zhang X, Li J. Sparse Bayesian multidimensional item response

theory modeling. arXiv preprint arXiv:2310.17820. 2023

[21] Wang C, Zhang S, Zhou Y. A comprehensive survey on deep learning-based cognitive diagnostic models. arXiv preprint arXiv:2407.05458. 2024

[22] Zhang L, Wu H, Jiang B. A reliability-aware framework for cognitive diagnosis. arXiv preprint arXiv:2401.10749. 2023

[23] Yan D, von Davier AA, Lewis C, editors. Computerized Multistage Testing: Theory and Applications. Roca Raton, New York: Chapman & Hall; 2014

[24] Liu Q, Zhuang Y, Bi H, Huang Z, Huang W, Li J, et al. Survey of computerized adaptive testing: A machine learning perspective. arXiv preprint arXiv:2404.00712. 2024

[25] Feng W, Ghosh A, Sireci S, Lan AS. Balancing test accuracy and security in computerized adaptive testing. arXiv preprint arXiv:2305.18312. 2023. Published May 18, 2023

[26] Wang H, Long T, Yin L, Zhang W, Xia W, Hong Q, et al. GMOCAT: A graph-enhanced multi-objective method for computerized adaptive testing. arXiv preprint arXiv: 2310.07477. 2023

Chapter 2

Psychometric Network Analysis: An Alternative Approach to Understanding Psychosocial Systems

María Inés Acuña and Silvina Alejandra Brussino

Abstract

This chapter examines psychometric network analysis (PNA), an innovative approach that conceptualizes psychological constructs as networks of interconnected variables. It emphasizes the importance of understanding the relationships among these variables, represented as nodes and edges in a network, to capture the complexity of psychological phenomena. The study highlights how researchers use PNA to analyze multivariate data collected at a single time point, particularly in psychometric assessments where they simultaneously assess multiple variables. PNA facilitates the exploration of conditional dependencies among variables, allowing researchers to visualize and interpret the intricate interactions within complex constructs such as political sophistication. Additionally, the chapter addresses the challenges associated with PNA, including the need for careful interpretation of causal relationships and the potential risk of overemphasizing psychometric analysis at the expense of the underlying theoretical frameworks. Ultimately, the chapter advocates for a balanced approach that integrates network analysis with traditional psychometric methods, fostering a deeper understanding of psychosocial constructs and their interactions while paving the way for future advancements in psychological networks.

Keywords: mereological model, psychometric network analysis, psychosocial phenomena, graphic Gaussian model, political sophistication

1. Introduction

In contemporary psychometrics, network models are valuable alternatives for understanding complex and multidimensional interactions [1]. A psychometric network uses network theory to represent the relationships between psychological variables, such as beliefs, attitudes, or personality traits. In such networks, nodes represent psychological variables, while edges denote the relationships or influences among them.

Psychometric networks thus significantly contribute to understanding the structural nature of psychological constructs as systems [2]. Additionally, they are beneficial for identifying patterns in behavior, content, beliefs, attitudes, and opinions [3], as well as other elements emerging from complex and dynamic interactions. Socially acquired characteristics shape these interactions, embedding them within diverse cultural contexts, as evident in psychosocial processes.

In this context, considering network approaches as an alternative to classical psychometric perspectives is particularly relevant, as they provide an innovative framework for capturing the complexity of psychological constructs. This approach enables their conceptualization and operational modeling as integrated systems through a detailed analysis of their elements, interactions, and functions within the network. Rather than attributing system dynamics to a single component or construct, the network approach assumes that such dynamics emerge from collective interactions organized within a network structure functioning as a complex whole. Consequently, network models significantly expand the possibilities of achieving a more comprehensive understanding of interactions in study designs and for specific groups within a research context exam [2, 4].

Over the past few decades, notable progress in psychometrics has established network models as a mereological approach, complementing latent models with an emphasis on specific variance between pairs [2, 5, 6]. Furthermore, theoretical, methodological, and technological advances, alongside open and free access to academic resources, materials, and software programs, reflect a continuous commitment to exploring the potential and overcoming the challenges of this expanding approach [4, 7].

Traditionally, the design and adaptation of techniques to measure attitudes, biases, cognition, values, political ideology, polarization, and other psychosocial variables rely on standardized procedures based on latent models [8, 9]. These models do not always align conceptually, statistically, or empirically [2, 10, 11]. Numerous instrumental studies hypothesize constructs based on formative or reflective parameters without recognizing the systemic nature of the theoretical model [12]. As a result, unidimensional and bidimensional models proposed for the same scale often reflect contextual variability and a mereological relationship among their elements (e.g., need for cognition, cognitive reflection, and political extremism). Statistical modeling of constructs while avoiding the pragmatic nihilism noted by Fried [13] requires reconciling conceptual substance with statistical criteria (e.g., modification criteria such as cross-loadings or covariance between unique factors) [5, 14].

Borsboom and Borsboom et al. [14, 15] addresses this issue by highlighting the frequent confusion between statistical and scientific inference in psychometrics. He argues that equating statistical models with substantive theoretical objectives reduces inferential purposes to mere model parameterization, reducing theoretical constructs to a secondary role. Network theory provides substantive interpretations and specifications that explain phenomena through the interaction of their components. The network model conceptualizes constructs as interconnected networks, wherein changes in one element or context induce alterations in system-wide interactions. Fundamentally, network analysis offers a robust exploratory framework to shape construct structures based on empirical data. This approach allows a more comprehensive and dynamic understanding by integrating theory with methodological and statistical decisions.

2. Psychometric network analysis

Psychometric network analysis (PNA) redefines the construct as a "network construct." It examines multivariate structures by integrating statistical models that facilitate the estimation, description, and evaluation of stability and accuracy in estimation [16, 17]. A network (or graph in mathematical literature) is an abstract representation of a system consisting of entities or variables known as nodes connected by edges. Nodes may represent various elements, such as individuals, symptoms, or evaluative reactions, while edges symbolize relationships, such as friendships, information flows, associations, or direct causal connections. The defining characteristics of psychometric networks include two points: (1) nodes represent variable estimates, and (2) covariance among indicators is interpreted as the outcome of direct interactions within the network. This approach enables the identification of conditional dependency patterns and their role within the system while also reducing statistical complexity through visual representation [14, 16, 18].

Borsboom and colleagues [2] identified three study designs commonly found in social sciences where psychometric network analysis (PNA) can be effectively applied: cross-sectional networks, longitudinal networks utilizing panel data, and time-series networks. In cross-sectional networks, PNA aims to reveal the multivariate patterns of conditional dependencies that define the joint distribution of variables at various levels of aggregation. The applicable statistical procedures for this data type include the Ising model, the Gaussian graphical model (GGM), and the mixed graphical model (MGM). The Ising model uses raw data as input, the GGM utilizes the variance-covariance or correlation matrix, and the MGM also works with raw data [19].

In the panel data design, a limited set of repeated measures reflects both the association structure of variables at specific time points and how these conditional dependencies evolve. This design can help clarify the structure of individual differences and intra-individual changes simultaneously. The statistical procedure typically used for this data type is the multilevel graphical vector autoregression [2, 19].

Lastly, time-series data, which can encompass one or multiple individuals, illustrate the multivariate dependencies among the time series of variables assessed within individuals. Researchers most commonly employ PNA in scenarios aimed at understanding the dynamic structure of systems. Like the panel data design, the statistical procedure used for time-series data is also the multilevel graphical vector autoregression. While cross-sectional data can be analyzed independently using assumptions that allow for population-sample logic, time-series data necessitate a model that accounts for dependencies between data points [2]. Additionally, it is important to consider that the input matrix depends on the specific estimation routines used in R packages (e.g., psychonetrics, qgraph) for analyzing each model [2, 19].

In cross-sectional research designs, PNA utilizes data collected at a single time point, where edges represent conditional associations among simultaneously measured variables within a large sample. This approach helps study the psychometric test structure and analyze multiple variables from questionnaire data [14].

A network derived from cross-sectional multivariate data represents the pairwise Markov random fields (PMRF) model, which captures the joint probability distribution of variables in an undirected network [2, 20, 21]. In PMRF, nodes (circles) represent variables, and edges indicate conditional associations, which can be positive or negative. Blue, green, and red lines typically represent these associations. If other variables in the network fully explain the relationship between two variables, the model depicts the nodes as disconnected. Researchers estimate PMRF using Gaussian graphical models (GGM), which parameterize network edges as partial correlation coefficients for continuous data. The Ising model is used for binary data to parameterize edges as log-linear relationships. They can combine these into mixed graphical models (MGM), where they parameterize edges as coefficients in a generalized linear regression model to incorporate different data types [1, 22].

The interpretation of PMRF networks can be in various ways: as a statistical modeling framework, a representation of predictive relationships, a tool for identifying causal structures through conditional independencies, or an exploratory tool for understanding relationships without assuming a specific causal model. However, these interpretative possibilities can be incompatible and may conflict when research questions lack clarity. Therefore, if the goal is to examine the correlational structure, the analytical methodology must differ from that used to analyze system dynamics [21].

The PNA procedure consists of three sequential phases: (a) estimation of network structure, (b) description of network characteristics, and (c) stability and centrality assessment. In the first phase, node selection depends on substantive conceptual criteria, while edge selection depends on statistical theory applied to estimate conditional associations [23, 24].

In the GGM or partial correlation model, due to sample variations and the rarity of exact zero matrices, statistical regularization techniques such as Least Absolute Shrinkage and Selection Operator (LASSO) are required [25]. This technique estimates a range of networks, requiring optimization of data fit, for which the Extended Bayesian Information Criterion (EBIC) is recommended [26]. Finally, the EBICglasso function calculates the sparse graphical model using an EBIC-based tuning parameter and uses the Fruchterman-Reingold algorithm for the network visualization [16, 24, 27].

The second phase includes a topological description of the network, focusing on global features (e.g., density, dispersion) and local centrality features (e.g., strength, closeness) [18, 24]. Although social network models employ centrality measures such as betweenness, closeness, and strength in psychological networks, researchers should consider metrics that analyze the specific role of nodes. These metrics include expected influence, node predictability, stabilization, communication, strength, and closeness [2, 24]. These measures offer a different perspective on a node's role, making them helpful in addressing various research questions [28].

In the final phase, attention is paid to the consistency of parameter estimates across different samples because network parameters, edge weights, and centrality indices are subject to sampling variation. Researchers consider network estimation stable when it produces similar results with new samples, and they estimate precision by examining how closely the values approximate the true population parameters. Thus, larger sample sizes would allow more precise estimates. Ultimately, stability and precision checks require validation using bootstrapping or Bayesian sampling methods to assess and visualize uncertainty around parameter estimates. However, despite the use of these procedures, we should consider that model conditions may introduce an additional level of variability, complicating the interpretation of these estimates [23, 24, 29]. In the final phase, attention is paid to the consistency of parameter estimates across different samples because network parameters, edge weights, and centrality indices are subject to sampling variation. From this perspective, researchers consider network estimation stable when it produces results similar to those of new samples. They estimate precision by comparing estimated values to the true population parameters.

Thus, larger sample sizes would allow more precise estimates. Ultimately, stability and precision checks require validation using bootstrapping or Bayesian sampling methods to assess and visualize uncertainty around parameter estimates. However, despite the use of these procedures, we should consider that model conditions may introduce an additional level of variability, complicating the interpretation of these estimates [23, 24, 29].

3. Networks and psychosocial systems

As previously noted, approaching constructs from the psychometric network perspective involves considering specifications and interpretations related to systems as complex structures with properties of homeostatic property clusters.

That is, structures whose elements tend to cluster due to underlying causal processes, resulting in groupings that are not entirely deterministic but probabilistic and consistent [13].

Thus, we will focus on three of the most relevant network developments in social psychology. One is the Causal Attitude Network model, which conceptualizes attitudes as complex networks of interconnected evaluative reactions. In this perspective, researchers do not see attitudes as unidimensional entities but as networks of evaluative reactions toward an attitude object, such as beliefs, feelings, and behaviors. These reactions are interrelated and can influence each other [30].

On the other hand, the theory of belief dynamics (the Theory of Individual and Social-Level Belief Dynamics) posits that personal and social beliefs are interconnected. Furthermore, the quest to reduce dissonance corresponds to an increase in consistency between personal beliefs and the beliefs of the social group [3]. Finally, the Attitudinal Entropy Framework is a conceptual framework that seeks to understand individual attitudes through an approach based on information theory and thermodynamics. The AE theory has significant psychological implications, offering a new approach to studying how individuals form, change, and maintain attitudes. By understanding attitudes as dynamic systems seeking equilibrium, researchers can develop more effective strategies to address issues such as ambivalence and decisional conflict in decision-making [31].

These theories are supported by empirical studies on these dynamics concerning phenomena such as group consensus, polarization, radicalization, minority influence, political orientations, attitudes, voting decisions, and political communication, among others that benefit from a mereological approach in their analysis [32–36].

3.1 Political sophistication networks (PS)

This section explores the concept of PS from the network model through a mereological analysis of its structure. Researchers must account for conceptual and instrumental diversity and incorporate more frequent measurement models to analyze multivariate patterns of dependence and node relevance in two subsamples. Data obtained within the framework of a political culture study with probabilistic samples from two cities in Argentina are considered for this purpose [37].

Over six decades ago, literature on political behavior began to incorporate PS, highlighting key relationships and effects in various models proposed by social sciences and political psychology [38–42]. However, there is no consensus on its precise definition and appropriate measurement methods.

To organize these conceptual possibilities, Gallina [41] categorizes PS around two axes: a cognitive-pragmatic one and one related to the internal-external source.

The first axis includes notions that address how the political world is understood and what knowledge about politics is. Although both aim to understand how politically sophisticated thinking is acquired, the former focuses on the cognitive organization of information. At the same time, the latter emphasizes the amount of information that gives meaning to the quality of thought. On the second axis, Gallina suggests considering, on the one hand, notions from internal sources, such as beliefs in one's abilities and political interest, and, on the other, those that highlight the influence of external factors like media, civic education, and the role of political parties. The resulting categories are PS approaches: expert, educational, psychological, and mobilization.

In the field of political psychology in Argentina, two pragmatic approaches to PS predominate: one integrates cognitive-motivational elements of knowledge (PK) and political interest (PI) [43–47], while the other proposes a bidimensional model based on conceptual differentiation and integration, excluding indicators of political interest [48, 49], based on latent psychometric approaches. Furthermore, the interactions between knowledge, interests, and beliefs about the self, along with other elements that form part of the personality system from a socio-cognitive perspective [50, 51], are consistent with the conceptual logic put forward in the mereological perspective. In this sense, we propose considering a network model of SP that includes PK, PI, sources of political efficacy (PE), internal (IPE), external (EPE), and the source of consumption of political information (CPI).

Data were collected using: (a) the Political Knowledge Scale [45], comprised of eight items on political and civic knowledge (e.g., I2: "What is the decision-making body regarding the constitutionality of laws?"). Responses were scored as follows: 0 (incorrect), 1 (partially correct), and 2 (correct). (b) The Political Interest Scale [44, 46] consisted of six items assessing interest in political processes or their outcomes (e.g., PI3: "I am interested in learning how political parties operate"). Responses ranged from 1 (strongly disagree) to 5 (strongly agree). (c) The Internal and External Political Efficacy Scale (IPE, EPE) [44, 46] showed two dimensions: the first recorded IPE by evaluating beliefs in one's ability to influence political matters, using four items (e.g., IPE4: "I could perform as well as anyone else in a political position"), with a five-point response format ranging from 1 (strongly disagree) to 5 (strongly agree). The second dimension, EPE, included four items assessing beliefs about the government's capacity to address political issues (e.g., EPE2: "How much attention do you think the government pays to what people think when making decisions?"), with a response format ranging from 1 (not at all) to 5 (a lot). (d) For CPI, we assessed the frequency of exposure by source (television, radio, newspaper, and web) for the consumption of political information.

Using a probabilistic sample, we explored the relationship between elements in two subsamples corresponding to capital cities in southern Patagonia and northern Argentina: n = 462 from Neuquén and n = 419 from Salta. Based on the data, we analyzed the GGM model and estimated the inverse covariance matrix, assuming that unobserved latent variables do not cause observed covariances between variables [52]. The networks in **Figures 1** and **2** represent a GGM we estimated using the qgraph R package available in JASP (Version 0.19). We applied the EBICglasso regularization method with a gamma hyperparameter set to $\gamma = .05$ to remove spurious edges. We generated the network layout using the Fruchterman-Reingold algorithm, which arranges the graph in a spring-embedded model. Finally, we conducted nonparametric bootstrapping with a sample of N = 1000 [19, 24].

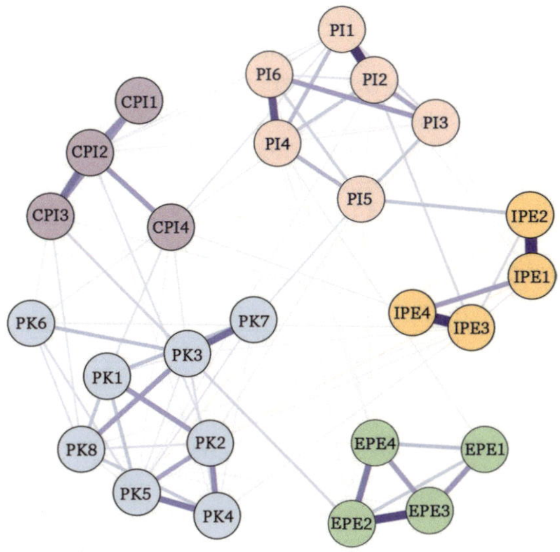

Figure 1.
This figure illustrate the regularized partial correlation networks for Neuquén. Solid-blue edges represent positive, regularized partial correlations. No specific minimum, maximum, or cutoff values were used. Edge weights in the separated network reached a maximum of 0.60 (IPE1–IPE2) and 0.53 (IPE3–IPE4).

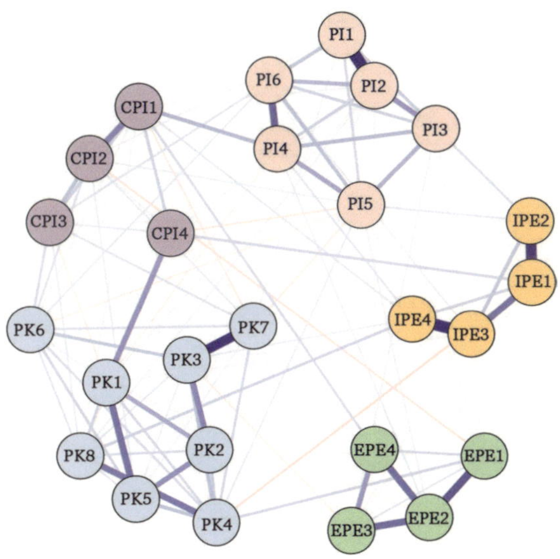

Figure 2.
This figure illustrate the regularized partial correlation networks for Salta. Solid-blue edges represent positive, regularized partial correlations. No specific minimum, maximum, or cutoff values were used. Edge weights in the separated network reached a maximum of 0.60 (IPE1–IPE2) and 0.53 (IPE3–IPE4).

3.1.1 PNA results

In **Figure 1**, 140 non-null edges were observed among 26 nodes, whereas in **Figure 2**, the connected nodes totaled 153, indicating that the network corresponding to Salta exhibited greater structural density than Neuquén. However, the interactions represented in both cases reached high interaction values (≥.35) [53], with estimates of 0.60 and 0.53, respectively. Bootstrapping plots reflect varying confidence intervals, suggesting results and centrality estimates that should be cautiously treated [19, 24].

The networks exhibited clustering tendencies with weak or absent direct interactions between nodes from different constructs. Moderate to strong interactions were observed among elements within the same construct. IPE1 and IPE2 nodes (general political competence) and IPE3 and IPE4 (political positions) displayed the strongest and closest interactions in the network. Regarding political knowledge (PK) content, both networks visually identified the proximity between elements concerning partisan groups: PK7 (i.e., the party to which the mayor belongs) and PK3 (i.e., the party with the most representatives in the provincial legislature). EPE nodes exhibited no significant interactions with nodes from other groups in the estimated network.

In **Figure 1**, PI5, EPI2, and EPI1 nodes shared references to specific campaign/political positions. The moderate interaction between CP4 (web) and CP3 (newspapers) may be due to the overlap between reading print newspapers and reading newspapers online and listening to traditional radio and online radio. In **Figure 2**, interest in political news (PI4) is directly connected to consumption via television (CPI1) and indirectly through newspapers (CP3). Conditional relationships between elements suggest that, in the network shown in **Figure 1**, interest in listening to or watching political news (PI4) and engaging in political discussions (PI1) are predicted by each other when controlling for interest in reading political information (PI6).

In the network, corresponding to **Figure 2**, conditional independence is found between the belief that holding elections makes the government pay more attention

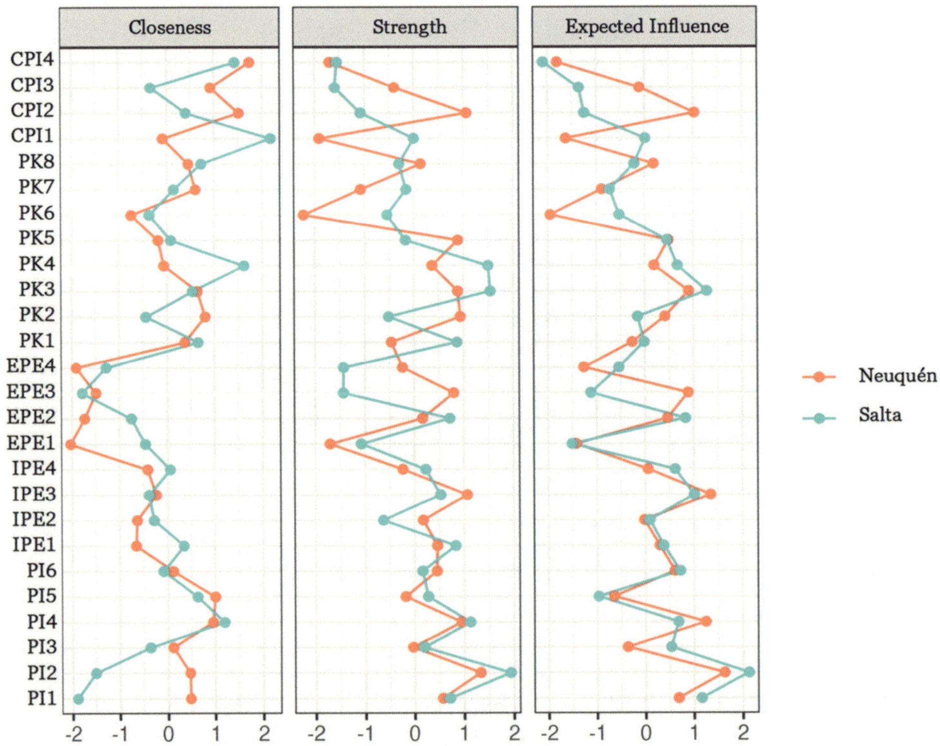

Figure 3.
Centrality plots of SP networks for Neuquén and Salta.

to public opinion (EPE1) and the belief that government actions improve people's well-being (EPE4), given the beliefs about the actual attention paid by the government (EPE2).

Additionally, the centrality indices presented in **Figure 3** suggest that, for both networks, the relevance of PI, PK, and PE content is important for an SP network. Here, elements are interdependent due to homeostatic or logical reasons (e.g., if there is interest in political conversations, political news also becomes interesting; or if there is a personal assessment of competence to hold a political position, there is also a belief in one's competence to participate politically). The focus is not on the specific values of these estimates but on how the visualization and dynamic conceptualization of elements reflect the behavioral tendencies and variabilities inherent to the phenomena.

4. Final remarks

Sensitivity to cultural differences and situational contexts is crucial in studying psychosocial phenomena, whether in the instrumental phases of design and adaptation or those aimed at estimating changes, predictive assessments, or hypothesis generation. In this regard, including the network psychometrics approach (PNA) as an analytical strategy allows variability to be considered a logical criterion. Far from compromising validity evidence, this perspective integrates variability within a framework of coherence between the theorized characteristics of the construct in a specific context and statistical estimates. In other words, it allows the convergence of scientific and statistical inferences. So, variability is integrated as a key criterion alongside substantive criteria when optimizing decisions, such as discarding or modifying the wording of an item in a test, complemented by statistical criteria (e.g., discrimination index, MSA) and inquiry conditions, such as order effects in psychosocial processes and phenomena. Particularly useful for instrumental decisions are centrality indices for identifying evaluative reactions with the most significant impact on the construct analyzed, such as PI2, PK3, and others, and enabling comparisons between different samples.

In this case, when considering, for example, the strength of each node in the two networks, a trend toward greater relevance is found in elements that directly state the content of the construct. Of the six items that make up the PI Scale, both networks highlight: "I am usually interested in political matters" and "I find it interesting to listen to or watch news about politics" (PI2 and PI4). In the Neuquén SP network, "I feel competent to participate in politics" (IPE3) and the belief that one's opinion exerts some influence on government decisions (EPE3), while in the Salta network, the belief about how much attention the government pays to people's opinions in its decisions (EPE2) stands out.

On the other hand, nodes related to PK that maintain direct and strong or moderate connections correspond to evaluations of specific contents, such as the party with the majority of members in the legislative branch, the body responsible for deciding constitutional laws, those responsible for appointing Supreme Court judges, and the body sanctioning provincial laws (PK2–PK5). This condition suggests that PK content could correspond to specific categories needing review. However, a cautious attitude is imperative when facing the disconnection of certain elements, as this could suggest an overestimation or underestimation of the role played by each element.

As traditional elements of the latent SP approach, responses linked to PI and PK show no direct interactions. In contrast, from the network approach, SP scores could be interpreted as the effects of the interaction between interests, knowledge of the functioning of the political system, and beliefs in political efficacy. Future studies, including aspects such as party affiliation, modes of participation, and other elements suggested in Gallina's categorization [41], could provide insights into our understanding of this system. Finally, the recurrence of political information consumption within PI elements suggests that its inclusion as an indicator or variable may not be relevant.

We acknowledge the limitations of using data collected in a study not aligned with the underlying theory or network model during its planning phase. Additionally, there are inherent restrictions to using self-reports and the impossibility of comparing structures, dynamics, and conclusions related to the elements considered in SP networks. We have not identified any previous studies on SP developed using a network-based methodological approach.

In this sense, the development and advancement of the PNA, in continuous dialog with the latent psychometric model, allows the recognition of instrumental and inferential problems inherent to social and political psychology, considering that dimensionality variations often result from covariance between unique factors due to the interactive and mereological nature of the elements.

In other words, the possibility of integrating reflective and mereological procedures to understand psychosocial phenomena not only leads to improved instrumental decisions but also to the conceptual and theoretical substance of such phenomena. In addition, considering the influence of variability through the estimation of interactive effects (e.g., biases, social desirability) will result in a more comprehensive understanding of models and their statistical adjustments.

However, we must address two significant challenges. The first lies in achieving an appropriate balance as knowledge of psychometric networks broadens. On the one hand, this balance involves avoiding hasty judgments or generalizations and, on the other, accepting uncertainty, following Cooper's recommendation to adopt a reflective, self-critical attitude open to new perspectives [54]. The second challenge is related to the caution necessary to prevent network analysis from overshadowing network theory, just as latent variable modeling has sometimes overshadowed the underlying theory of these variables, as pointed out by Borsboom [14].

Therefore, in researching psychosocial constructs, we consider the limitations and observations highlighted by Marsman and Rhemtulla of notable value [55]. These emphasize the critical aspects of network analysis, such as the causal interpretation of relationships that, in many cases, are not genuinely causal, inferences derived from the absence of edges fixed at zero through regularization procedures, and the predominantly exploratory nature of networks.

Acknowledgements

We acknowledge and thank the National Scientific System, particularly CONICET and Argentina's public universities, whose support policies for scientific knowledge generation have enabled our research.

Conflict of interest

The authors declare no conflict of interest.

Author details

María Inés Acuña[1]* and Silvina Alejandra Brussino[2]

1 National University of Comahue, Neuquén, Argentina

2 Institute of Psychological Research, CONICET-National University of Córdoba, Argentina

*Address all correspondence to: maria.acuna@face.uncoma.edu.ar

References

[1] Epskamp S, Maris G, Waldorp LJ, Borsboom D. Network psychometrics. In: Irwing P, Booth T, Hughes DJ, editors. The Wiley Handbook of Psychometric Testing: A Multidisciplinary Reference on Survey, Scale and Test Development. Hoboken, New Jersey, USA: Wiley Blackwell; 2018. pp. 953-986. DOI: 10.1002/9781118489772.ch30

[2] Borsboom D, Deserno MK, Rhemtulla M, Epskamp S, Fried EI, McNally RJ, et al. Network analysis of multivariate data in psychological science. Nature Reviews Methods Primers. 2021;**1**:58. DOI: 10.1038/s43586-021-00055-w

[3] Dalege J, Galesic M, Olsson H. Networks of beliefs: An integrative theory of individual- and social-level belief dynamics. Psychological Review. 2024:253-290. DOI: 10.1037/rev0000494

[4] Psychosystems. Psychosystems.org [Internet]. Available from: http://psychosystems.org

[5] Edwards JR, Bagozzi RP. On the nature and direction of relationships between constructs and measures. Psychological Methods. 2000;**5**(2):155-174. DOI: 10.1037/1082-989X.5.2.155

[6] Marsman M, Borsboom D, Kruis J, Epskamp S, van Bork R, Waldorp LJ, et al. An introduction to network psychometrics: Relating Ising network models to item response theory models. Multivariate Behavioral Research. 2018;**53**(1):15-35. DOI: 10.1080/00273171.2017.1379379

[7] Psychonetrics. Psychonetrics.org [Internet]. Available from: http://psychonetrics.org

[8] International Test Commission. The ITC Guidelines for Translating and Adapting Tests [Internet]. 2nd ed. 2017. Available from: www.InTestCom.org

[9] Comparative Survey Design and Implementation [Internet]. Available from: https://ccsg.isr.umich.edu

[10] Markus KA, Borsboom D. Frontiers of Test Validity Theory: Measurement, Causation, and Meaning. 2nd ed. New York: Routledge; 2020

[11] Haslbeck JMB, Ryan O, Robinaugh DJ, Waldorp LJ, Borsboom D. Modeling psychopathology: From data models to formal theories. Psychological Methods. 2022;**27**(6):930-957. DOI: 10.1037/met0000303

[12] Finn A, Wang L. Formative vs. reflective measures: Facets of variation. Journal of Business Research. 2013;**66**(6):861-867. DOI: 10.1016/j.jbusres.2012.08.001

[13] Fried EI. What are psychological constructs? On the nature and statistical modelling of emotions, intelligence, personality traits and mental disorders. Health Psychology Review. 2017;**11**(2):130-134. DOI: 10.1080/17437199.2017.1306718

[14] Borsboom D. Possible futures for network psychometrics. Psychometrika. 2022;**87**(1):253-265. DOI: 10.1007/s11336-022-09851-z

[15] Borsboom D, Cramer AOJ, Fried EI, Isvoranu AM, Robinaugh DJ, Dalege J, et al. Chapter 1. Network perspectives. In: Isvoranu AM, Epskamp S, Waldorp LJ, Borsboom D, editors. Network Psychometrics with R: Guide for Behavioral and Social Scientists. New

York: Routledge, Taylor & Francis Group; 2022. pp. 1-21

[16] Epskamp S. Network psychometrics [dissertation]. Amsterdam: University of Amsterdam; 2017

[17] Isvoranu AM, Epskamp S, Waldorp L, Borsboom D, editors. Network Psychometrics with R: A Guide for Behavioral and Social Scientists. New York: Taylor & Francis; 2022

[18] Deserno MK, Isvoranu AM, Epskamp S, Blanken TF. Chapter 3. Descriptive analyses of network structures. In: Isvoranu AM, Epskamp S, Waldorp LJ, Borsboom D, editors. Network Psychometrics with R: A Guide for Behavioral and Social Scientists. New York: Routledge, Taylor & Francis Group; 2022. pp. 41-60

[19] Burger J, Isvoranu A-M, Lunansky G, Haslbeck JMB, Epskamp S, Hoekstra RHA, et al. Reporting standards for psychological network analyses in cross-sectional data. Psychological Methods. 2023;**28**(4):806-824. DOI: 10.1037/met0000471

[20] Lauritzen SL. Graphical Models, Oxford Statistical Science Series. Oxford: Clarendon Press; 1996

[21] Epskamp S, Haslbeck JMB, Isvoranu AM, Van Borkulo CD. Chapter 6. Pairwise Markov random fields. In: Isvoranu AM, Epskamp S, Waldorp LJ, Borsboom D, editors. Network Psychometrics with R: A Guide for Behavioral and Social Scientists. New York: Routledge, Taylor & Francis Group; 2022. pp. 81-100

[22] Epskamp S, van Borkulo CD, van der Veen DC, Servaas MN, Isvoranu AM, Riese H, et al. Personalized network modeling in psychopathology: The importance of contemporaneous and temporal connections. Clinical Psychological Science: A Journal of the Association for Psychological Science. 2018;**6**(3):416-427. DOI: 10.1177/2167702617744325

[23] Epskamp S, Borsboom D, Fried EI. Estimating psychological networks and their accuracy: A tutorial paper. Behavior Research Methods. 2018;**50**:195-212. DOI: 10.3758/s13428-017-0862-1

[24] Isvoranu AM, Epskamp S. Which estimation method to choose in network psychometrics? Deriving guidelines for applied researchers. Psychological Methods. 2023;**28**(4):925-946. DOI: 10.1037/met0000439

[25] Friedman JH, Hastie T, Tibshirani R. Sparse inverse covariance estimation with the graphical lasso. Biostatistics. 2008;**9**(3):432-441. DOI: 10.1093/biostatistics/kxm045

[26] Chen J, Chen Z. Extended Bayesian information criteria for model selection with large model spaces. Biometrika. 2008;**95**(3):759-771. DOI: 10.1093/biomet/asn034

[27] Isvoranu AM, Epskamp S. Chapter 4. Constructing and drawing networks in qgraph. In: Isvoranu AM, Epskamp S, Waldorp LJ, Borsboom D, editors. Network Psychometrics with R: A Guide for Behavioral and Social Scientists. New York: Routledge, Taylor & Francis Group; 2022

[28] Letina S, Blanken TF, Deserno MK, Borsboom D. Expanding network analysis tools in psychological networks: Minimal spanning trees, participation coefficients, and motif analysis applied to a network of 26 psychological attributes. Complexity. 2019;**2019**:1-27. DOI: 10.1155/2019/9424605

[29] Fried EI, Epskamp S, Veenman M, van Borkulo CD. Chapter 8. Network stability, comparison, and replicability. In: Isvoranu AM, Epskamp S, Waldorp LJ, Borsboom D, editors. Network Psychometrics with R: A Guide for Behavioral and Social Scientists. New York: Routledge, Taylor & Francis Group; 2022

[30] Dalege J, Borsboom D, van Harreveld F, van den Berg H, Conner M, van der Maas HL. Toward a formalized account of attitudes: The causal attitude network (CAN) model. Psychological Review. 2016;**123**(1):2-22. DOI: 10.1037/a0039802

[31] Dalege J, Borsboom D, van Harreveld F, Lunansky G, van der Maas HLJ. The attitudinal entropy (AE) framework: Clarifications, extensions, and future directions. Psychological Inquiry. 2018;**29**(4):218-228. DOI: 10.1080/1047840X.2018.1542235

[32] van der Maas HLJ, Dalege J, Waldorp L. The polarization within and across individuals: The hierarchical Ising opinion model. Journal of Complex Networks. 2020;**8**(2):cnaa010. DOI: 10.1093/comnet/cnaa010

[33] Chambon M, Dalege J, Elberse JE, van Harreveld F. A psychological network approach to attitudes and preventive behaviors during pandemics: A COVID-19 study in the United Kingdom and the Netherlands. Social Psychological and Personality Science. 2022;**13**(1):233-245. DOI: 10.1177/19485506211002420

[34] Lind AV, Morton TA, Dalege J. Comparing attitudinal structures between political orientations: A network analysis of climate change attitudes. Journal of Environmental Psychology. 2024;**97**:102370. DOI: 10.1016/j.jenvp.2024.102370

[35] Dalege J, Borsboom D, van Harreveld F, van der Maas HLJ. Network structure explains the impact of attitudes on voting decisions. Scientific Reports. 2017;7:4909. DOI: 10.1038/s41598-017-05048-y

[36] Hopp T. A network analysis of political incivility dimensions. Communication and the Public. 2019;**4**(3):204-223. DOI: 10.1177/2057047319877278

[37] Brussino S, Imhoff D, Paz García A, Alonso D, Rabbia H, Dreizik M, et al. Heterogeneidades y policromías de las culturas políticas locales. Indagación psico-política de los casos de Salta, Córdoba y Neuquén (Argentina). Revista SAAP. 2021;**15**(1):183-210. DOI: 10.46468/rsaap.15.1.N2

[38] Campbell A, Converse PE, Miller WE, Stokes DE. The American Voter. Chicago: University of Chicago Press; 1960

[39] Dalton R. The representation gap and political sophistication: A contrarian perspective. Comparative Political Studies. 2021;**54**(5):889-917. DOI: 10.1177/0010414020957673

[40] Vitriol JA, Sandor J, Vidigal R, Farhart C. On the independent roles of cognitive & political sophistication: Variation across attitudinal objects. Applied Cognitive Psychology. 2023;**37**(2):319-331. DOI: 10.1002/acp.4022

[41] Gallina M. The concept of political sophistication: Labeling the unlabeled. Political Studies Review. 2023;**21**(4):836-846. DOI: 10.1177/14789299221146058

[42] Valli C, Eugster B, Arlt D. The more sophisticated, the more biased? Testing a new measure of political sophistication on biased information processing.

International Journal of Public Opinion Research. 2023;**35**(4):edad037. DOI: 10.1093/ijpor/edad037

[43] Alonso D, Brussino S. Political system justification in Argentina: Ideology, system performance, and the legitimization of democracy. Psykhe. 2024;**33**(2):1-22. DOI: 10.7764/psykhe.2022.48975

[44] Brussino S, Sorribas PM, Gutiérrez J, Imhoff D, Kerman L, Medrano L, et al. Participación política en jóvenes: Un análisis descriptivo. In: XIII Jornadas de Investigación y Segundo Encuentro de Investigadores en Psicología del Mercosur. Buenos Aires: Facultad de Psicología - Universidad de Buenos Aires; 2006

[45] Brussino S, Sorribas P, Medrano L. Características psicométricas de la medición del conocimiento político. Revista Iberoamericana de Diagnostico y Evaluacion Psicologica. 2008;**25**(1):179-192

[46] Brussino S, Rabbia HH, Sorribas P. Perfiles sociocognitivos de la participación política de los jóvenes. Revista Interamericana de Psicología. 2009;**43**(2):279-287

[47] Acuña M, Brussino S. El efecto de las emociones políticas en las elecciones participativas de los jóvenes: Emociones políticas y toma de decisión [tesis doctoral]. Córdoba: Facultad de Psicología, Universidad Nacional de Córdoba; 2020

[48] Paz García P, Sorribas P, Taricco L, Danieli N, Gutiérrez M. Prácticas de consumo y dietas informativas ciudadanas. InMediaciones de la Comunicación. 2023;**18**(1):89-114. DOI: 10.18861/ic.2023.18.1.3302

[49] Sorribas PM, Paz Garcia AP, Maldonado LI. Sofisticación política: Contribuciones a la evaluación de su bidimensionalidad. Psicologia Política. 2023;**23**(58):536-555

[50] Bandura A, National Inst of Mental Health. Social Foundations of Thought and Action: A Social Cognitive Theory. Englewood Cliffs (NJ): Prentice-Hall; 1986

[51] Caprara GV, Vecchione M. Personality approaches to political behavior. In: Huddy L, Sears DO, Levy JS, editors. The Oxford Handbook of Political Psychology. 2nd ed. Oxford: Oxford University Press; 2013. pp. 23-58

[52] Epskamp S, Rhemtulla M, Borsboom D. Generalized network psychometrics: Combining network and latent variable models. Psychometrika. 2017;**82**(4):904-927. DOI: 10.1007/s11336-017-9557-x

[53] Christensen AP, Golino H. On the equivalency of factor and network loadings. Behavior Research Methods. 2021;**53**(4):1563-1580. DOI: 10.3758/s13428-020-01500-6

[54] Cooper H. Introduction: Objectives of psychological research and their relations to research methods. In: Cooper H, editor. APA Handbook of Research Methods in Psychology: Foundations, Planning, Measures, and Psychometrics. Vol. 1. Washington (DC): American Psychological Association; 2023. pp. 3-19

[55] Marsman M, Rhemtulla M. Guest editors' introduction to the special issue "network psychometrics in action": Methodological innovations inspired by empirical problems. Psychometrika. 2022;**87**(1):1-11. DOI: 10.1007/s11336-022-09861-x

Chapter 3

Ethnopsychometry: The Road to Valid, Reliable Yet Culturally Sensitive and Relevant Measures

Rolando Diaz-Loving, Sofia Rivera Aragon and Marcoantonio Villanueva Bustamante

Abstract

Following in the tradition of ethnopsychological research, this chapter delineates the process toward obtaining statistically and conceptually valid and reliable personality measures that, at the same time, are also culturally relevant and sensitive to the Mexican culture. To demonstrate if a trait has universal, regional, or local significance and meaning, a methodological approach is advanced that integrates universal constructs and measures with idiosyncratic local manifestations. This process addresses the following steps: (1) scan the literature for the conceptual and theoretical definition of a construct; (2) delineate dimensions and definitions ascribed to that construct; (3) identify all the measures of the construct; (4) describe the measures and their dimensions; (5) produce a matrix with all the measures and all their dimensions; (6) create a new integral definition; (7) conduct exploratory research in the target culture to identify the emotions, thoughts, and behaviors of the construct; (8) content analysis to identify the dimensions that describe the target construct in the selected cultural group; (9) create a new matrix with the dimensions from the measures from the literature and the ones obtained in the exploratory phase; (10) identify universal dimensions and idiosyncratic factors present in the target sample; (11) develop a new measuring instrument that includes the universal and idiosyncratic factors; and (12) apply the new instrument and do all the traditional validity and reliability tests. As an example of this process, theory and data of power in dyadic relationships will be presented.

Keywords: ethnopsychology, ethnopsychometry, measurement, validity, reliability, culture

1. Introduction

Following in the tradition of ethnopsychological research proposed by Díaz-Guerrero [1–5], this chapter delineates the process toward obtaining statistically and conceptually valid and reliable personality measures that, at the same time, are also culturally relevant and sensitive to the Mexican culture. To demonstrate

IntechOpen

if a trait has universal, regional or local significance and meaning, a new methodological approach is advanced that considers both an apparently universal construct and measure, as well as the idiosyncratic local manifestation. This process is specified in Diaz-Loving [6] and addresses the following steps: (1) scan the literature for the conceptual and theoretical definition of a construct; (2) create a table with all the dimensions and definitions ascribed to that construct; (3) identify all the measures created to measure the construct; (4) create a table with all the measures, their dimensions and operational definitions; (5) produce a matrix with all the measures on one axis and all their dimensions on the other axis; (6) create a new integral definition of the construct; (7) conduct exploratory research in the target culture (interviews, focus groups, free associations, multidimensional scaling, semantic networks, etc.) to identify the emotions, thoughts and behaviors of the target group to the selected construct; (8) do content analysis of the exploratory data to identify the dimensions that describe the target construct in the selected cultural group; (9) create a new matrix with the dimensions from the measures from the literature and the ones obtained in the exploratory phase; (10) identify universal dimensions (at least between the target culture and the cultures represented in the literature), idiosyncratic factors present in the target culture but not in the general literature, and pseudo universal dimensions present in the literature but not in the target culture; (11) develop a new measuring instrument that includes the universal and idiosyncratic factors; and (12) apply the new instrument in the culture representative sample and do all the traditional validity and reliability tests. As an example of this process, theory and data of power in dyadic relationships will be presented.

First, we reviewed the literature on the conceptual and theoretical definition of power. Power is present from the very moment of birth, and personal power implies reciprocal influence with other people. The newborn has power over the mother or those who care for him. For almost everyone, the first learning experience takes place within the family or the group, where power has been distributed, and complex reciprocal influences have been established between the means and processes of power. Power in close relationships refers to those who make decisions, raise ideas or solve problems, receive more agreement for their position, or participate more in discussions. It also includes the behavioral patterns to impose a position, and the strategies and styles a person uses during the interaction. Another important aspect to consider is the direction of power. Negotiation is a bilateral process of assuming power; both members can be involved in the decisions, or manipulation can be unilateral when only one member of the couple controls the situation [7].

French and Raven [8], when defining power, consider that there are two classes: relative and absolute power. They indicate that relative power is always circumstantial; it depends on the moment and is unstable because it is usually based on physical force and is based on fear. On the other hand, absolute power is stable across settings and situations and has an awe of legitimacy. Focusing more on interpersonal relationships, personal power is possessed by a single person; it can be of many kinds, and these can be combined with each other; a person can destroy, threaten, produce something, exchange, and achieve integration, which includes the power to be accepted, respected, loved, enjoy legitimacy, and be part of a larger network [9].

Throughout the psychological literature, the process of power constitutes a central theoretical concept in the analysis of a number of basic phenomena in psychology. This has impacted the number of definitions and dimensions ascribed to the construct. Next, a brief description of some proposals developed for the conceptualization of power is presented. The models are the basis for a clearer conceptualization of power in interpersonal relationships (**Table 1**).

Secondly, we identified all the measures created to measure the construct. As demonstrated in the definitions of power, the construct is multidimensional, and as a result, different measures often cover different dimensions. The main obstacle in

Thibaut and Kelley [10] Using theories of reinforcement and economic man, they organize the theory of behavioral exchange. They specify that in all social interactions, there is an implicit or explicit exchange of rewards or costs. They propose that power strategies are a way to achieve results in interpersonal situations through two processes: Increase. A powerful person provides rewards to induce another or perform desirable behaviors. Reduce: the actor applies negative sanctions in any case in which the other person behaves differently than intended. To explain power relations, they have considered two types of power: (A) destiny control, which occurs when A influences B to change his behavior but which does not affect his own outcome. (B) Behavior control is where A and B change their behavior according to their choice of both.
Cartwright and Alvin [11] It considers power as a symmetrical relationship where A influences B, but B also influences A. Power produces changes even if it is not related to influence; they mention a series of resources such as wealth, prestige, ability, information, physical strength, capacity for gratification. In such relationships, progressive feelings of frustration and hopelessness are observed in the two participants or in one of them.
Homans [12] Power is defined in two terms. Distributive Justice: the relationship between what people get in terms of reward and what it means in terms of costs, here and now. Status Congruence refers to the impression that the person makes on others of the stimuli that he or she presents to other people, which may affect his or her subsequent behavior and in relation to future consequences.
Etizioni [13] Distinguishes three basic types of power: (1) "coercive" power refers to physical means such as restrictions and control over basic needs (food, sex, comfort, etc.). (2) "Remunerative" power that is based on the satisfaction of material needs such as housing and other property. (3) "Normative" power rests on the manipulation of rewards and symbolic deprivations, such as esteem and disapproval.
Rodman [14] Describes four general states of power: Authoritarian, where one of the members has the necessary tools that are dependent on the functionality of the relationship; Modification of authority, where both members have equally important and valuable resources; Transitional egalitarianism, where there is no clear definition of which resources are identified with power, and this is distributed indistinctly, it is defined by the equitable and shared distribution of power.
Safilios and Rothschild [15] Schematizes personal power derived from resources and includes: socio-economic; love and affection, expressions of understanding and support, companionship, sex, and services.
Kenneth [16] Classifies power into three categories. Shared, compensatory, and conditional power. The approach refers to the general repercussions of the growth of man's knowledge and abilities on the complexities of the power structure.
Lewin [17] Field theory explains the influence and power in a functional relationship of A and B. Power is classified according to its nature by taking into account motivations, intensity of the forces of resistance, and degree of vigilance, for which three categories are suggested. (1) Positive and negative actions, resistance, and vigilance of authority. (2) Internalization of values and behaviors of authority. (3) Based on legitimacy, hierarchy, and the recognition of their superiors of being able to influence through assimilation.
Boulding [18] Distinguishes three classifications of power: (a) threatening power, (b) economic power, and (c) integrating power. It is closely related to another tripartite division of power to destroy, the power to produce, and the power to exchange love, respect, friendship, and legitimacy.

Table 1.
Definitions and descriptions of power in the psychological literature.

close relationship power research has been the lack of reliable and valid measurement techniques. Most studies have used self-reports of decision-making to determine the balance of power between the couple. This approach conceives of marital power as a function from which each member makes the majority of decisions in various and different areas.

Some studies have taken a different approach using observational procedures, usually taking the form of performing several tasks or conducting structured discussions and estimated by the researcher as behavioral indicators of power. Studies comparing both forms of measurement have shown little correspondence [19–23]. Another related problem is the small match between different measures of power of the same type [24] (Hadley and Jacob, 1973). The fact that there is no agreement in measures of the same type poses a serious problem that stems from conceptualization problems and is confirmed by an ambiguous and inconsistent measurement.

Only a few studies have used procedures that explicitly measure the ability to produce the effects set out in the definitions: measures of self-report often unite partners' perceptions of decision-makers, while observational measures focus on strategy for exclusion of outcomes or events.

In an attempt to distinguish between the different definitions, Olson and Cromwell [25] classified existing research on family power into three domains. Power bases relate to the sources or resources, such as knowledge or rewards that are possessed by family members that form the basis of control of one member over the other. Power processes refer to the direct observation and measurement of family interaction. These processes can also be delineated in terms of the amount of inference required by the observer. Some measures such as speaking time require simply noting the frequency or duration of a behavior, while others also include judgment about the quality of the event, that is, that one member is submissive to the other. etc. [26]. And finally, regarding the results of the use of power, these studies ask who makes decisions in various family aspects, and others examine the similarity between the couple's joint response to a specific problem.

In general, studies in the field have focused on decision-making [27]. This research reflects the effects of specific individual situations between husband and wife, which are of great importance for decision-making in the couple. Most of the studies on decision-making are based on the work of Blood and Wolfe [28], who measured marital power by asking wives which partner made the final decision in each of eight areas ranging from work opportunities to their financial life. The responses of 909 wives were used to categorize couples as in Lu's [29] study when it came to decision-making. These authors found that wives who reported a syncretic decision structure (i.e., both partners jointly made the decisions) also reported the highest levels of satisfaction, while those in whom the wife was dominant were less satisfied, and the group of spouses who dominated were in the middle of the aforementioned groups in terms of satisfaction. Because they found that wives in same-sex marriages were more satisfied than those in autonomous marriages (where only one partner made the decisions), these authors suggest that equality per se is less important to the satisfaction of wives who are considered for decision-making. The dominant wife, according to these authors, gains her power through her husband's marginality or abstinence from marriage, conditions that are unlikely to lead to her satisfaction.

In another study measuring decision-making, Centers et al. [30] compared the Blood and Wolfe scale with a new scale that included six additional areas of decision-making in an attempt to provide a better representation of decisions not traditionally included in the husband's domain. The distribution of decision-making types differed depending on the scale used. On average, the original scale indicated greater power for the spouses, while the revised scale indicated equal power for both spouses. Using the same four categories as Blood and Wolfe [28], Centers et al. [30] found that individuals who reported wife dominance in decision-making had lower levels of marital satisfaction than those in the other groups, those in autonomous relationships reported the highest levels of satisfaction followed by husband-dominant relationships and syncretic relationships.

Power outcomes studies differ from decision-making studies in that they are based on partner interaction rather than individual self-reporting, and both differ from process measures in that they focus primarily on outcomes, that is, which partner is more important in the final decision.

Sargent [31] argued that process studies identify how change occurs, while outcome research attempts to identify what the changes are. Gray-Little and Burks [32] add that research on power bases is related to the reason why one member of the family is able to control another. In other words, the domains of power bases, processes, and outcomes direct the determinants, nature, and effects of power, respectively. Two lines of research have emerged regarding the basis of power. While quantitative studies aim to better understand the balance of power between partners or the absolute level of power, qualitative studies are concerned with the type of power used. Lewin's conceptualization of power as a potential to induce consent or submission provides the impetus for the study of the bases of power [11, 17]. According to Lewin [17], the one who exercises power is able to create a force in the subject of power through the use of a range of sources that affect the need for satisfaction and the basis that motivates it.

The only systematic evidence of the relationship between power bases and marital satisfaction has been given by Raven et al. [33], whose study power bases were defined in terms of the spouses' perceptions of the motives underlying submission to their partner's wishes. The subjects were asked to indicate which of the five power bases identified by French and Raven [8] was their partners' predominant source of influence and also to estimate their marital satisfaction on a three-point scale. Referent power was the most chosen power base for the most satisfied and moderately satisfied subjects, while coercion was the most common basis for the least satisfied subjects.

The literature on power in close relationships favors situational variables, the foundation of power, who imposes their will, and areas of the interaction where the use of power is seen. An aspect that receives much less attention is the ways in which power is manifested. This refers to both the strategies used and the permanent styles that people have to influence their partner. In summary, power in couple relationships would be any active or passive behavior, be it physical, verbal, or symbolic, directed at influencing a close partner. This would include situation variables, the basis of the behavior, who directs it and who receives it, as well as the consistent selection of strategies or personality types that direct the production of the behaviors. Taking this into account, we will focus on studying power as a process, that is, as a strategy. As mentioned before, power strategies are ways people use to influence others. In other words, power strategies describe an active process of power that is being exercised. Many social scientists have been interested in understanding how the process works and have tended to develop systems for classifying the various ways people use to change each other's behavior. The most salient measures of power strategies are presented in **Table 2**.

French and Raven [8]	Etizioni [13]	Kelman [34]	Parsons [35]	Marwell and Schmitt [36]	Falbo and Peplau [37]	Rivera et al. [38]
Reward Induction			Induction	Promises Reward Positive stimuli Positive Alternative		Negotiation Reciprocity Exchange
				Affiliative Promising Duty as manipulation	Affiliative Withdraw affection	Affiliative Withdraw affection Sexual
Coercive	Coercive					Coercive
Expert		Trust	Persuasion	Expert	Persuasion Insinuation	Persuasion
Legitimate	Normative	Internalization		Moral plea		Normativity
Inform			Convince		Talk Reason	Reasoning
	Monetary reward					Monetary reward
		Identify with		Feelings		
Deterrence			Monetary reward	Threat Punishment (cease to reward de) Stimulate		Threat Punishment
					Petition Request	Assertiveness
						Authoritarianism Imposition

Table 2.
Differences and similarities between models of power strategies.

DOI: http://dx.doi.org/10.5772/intechopen.1010251

2. Exploratory research of power strategies in a Mexican sample

This section will review various qualitative studies carried out to determine the definition and categories of strategies and styles used to influence couples in the Mexican population.

In the first study to evaluate the concept of power in couple relationships, a semantic networks technique was used following the model proposed by Reyes [39], which is described below:

First, participants were asked to offer all the words they related to the concept of power. They were instructed to use any defining words they could think of, including adjectives, nouns, verbs, and adverbs. Then, participants were asked to order the words according to the expression that best defined the concept of power. To analyze the concept, the size of the network was delimited by taking the 15 words with the highest semantic weight. This procedure was conducted with a sample of 288 men and 306 women, ages 15–50 years old.

The results by sex show that power is defined by men in general as strength, money, command, dominance, responsibility, shared, security, authoritarianism, and love. In the case of junior high school men, power is conceptualized as the force granted by money, command, and dominance. For high school men, power continues to be a force that is granted by money and command but also includes responsibility, dominance, and security, and this group refers to words such as work, superiority, and control. For the men with college degrees, they continue to mention that power is strength and domination, which grants command and money, but they also add economy, struggle, and fulfillment, being the only group that refers to shared power.

In the case of women, power continues to be command, strength, authority, money, and domination, but they add will and love. In the case of junior high school women, they mention that power is love through which they can command, obtain strength, and have authority, money, and dominance. On the other hand, high school women remark that it is a command that gives money, authority, and strength and that love, responsibility, and trust must be present when referring to it. College women like men refer to strength as the most important concept, which entails command, dominance, money and insecurity, authority and love.

A second study was carried out using an open-ended questionnaire. 121 people were selected, of which 60 were women and 61 men. The age ranged from 25 to 60 years, with a mean age of 30.5 years. Most of the subjects had a bachelor's degree. This technique was used to allow participants to write down everything that the concept of power in the relationship meant to them. The person was asked the following question: What is power in the relationship for you?

Content analysis based on the Krippendorff technique [40] was applied to the responses. Through this analysis, those responses that were similar in terms of content were connected. Once the responses were appended together, 15 judges were asked to develop the categories for each group of responses.

The results indicate that the definition of power in men and women is related to authoritarianism and imposition in decision-making by the couple. However, this definition is more common in women than in men. On the other hand, as for the definition of power as interaction (joint decision-making) was proposed more by men than by women. Additionally, power as a manipulation strategy was suggested more by women than by men. Content analysis of the exploratory data to identify the dimensions that describe the construct.

For men, the detected dimensions were authoritarian-imposition, interactive and persuasive-manipulative. Authoritarian and imposition refer to having authority over one's partner, controlling and imposing one's will, and making decisions for the other. Interactive power indicates understanding, mutual decision-making, and the ability to solve conflicts. Finally, persuasive-manipulative indicates the capacity to persuade the other, influence their behavior, and manipulate-coerce the other one to the power broker's wishes. In the case of females, the same three dimensions appear; however, in their case, authoritarian includes dominating the relationship. Interactive power includes equity and negotiation, and manipulation is considered blackmail.

Each qualitative technique provided evidence about the concept of power; although they all generally come to a similar meaning, the open-ended questionnaire provided more information about the concept. However, the general literature, instead of providing an explicit definition of power, gives a description of the influence procedures used. For example, equating power with the frequency of "interruptions," "who speaks first," or "who speaks the most." Other power studies suggest agreeing on the definition of power as the capacity to produce intentional effects [25, 41–45]. However, all these definitions have been formulated in individualistic cultures [46].

In Mexico, Díaz Guerrero and Diaz Loving [47] mention that power is any type of behavior through which others are made to do what we as individuals want to be done, putting the final decision in our hands. These authors use free associations and find that power is money, wealth, authority, and command. In the qualitative studies described in the previous section, the subjects similarly indicate that power is authority. This definition was used by both men and women. However, the meaning given to authority differs since each one defines it in terms of the sexual role assigned to their gender.

Consistent with cultural-type patterns, men refer to authority as their own, and women refer to it as the imposition and control of others. Power, understood from its imposing aspect, characterized by the domination-submission modality, linked to the process of socialization and traditional norms -in the sense that the strategies used are learned early in life- precedes the definition made in this study based on a dichotomy where woman indicate that power is authority and that authority is submission (others are in control) while the man states that power is authority and that authority is dominance (he assumes power).

Consistent with the traditional gender stance, working outside the home and providing for the family was a man's obligation, and being at home and taking care of the husband and children was the woman's obligation. Under this patriarchal marital norm, wives possess little power to influence the decisions the husband makes. Despite this, marital roles and behaviors are currently changing thanks to the increase in women's participation in the workplace [48–50].

Other attributes given to power were the use of interaction and manipulation. The first is a bilateral way of assuming power (both are involved in the decisions), and the second is a unilateral way (only one member of the couple makes the decision). In the case of the definition of power as interaction, equity becomes manifest, where both members of the couple decide. This change is due to the fact that women are currently beginning to have intervention in decision-making, either because they have entered the field of paid work or because of the academic preparation obtained.

On the other hand, when we talk about power as manipulation, we are talking about persuasion and influence, as well as blackmail. This last meaning given to power is more used by women than by men. As for power strategies, where the behavioral style used to ensure that the partner agrees to a series of requests, studies by Falbo and Peplau [37] show sexual differences in the use of power strategies in intimate relationships in Anglo-Saxons.

The strategies frequently reported by men in Mexico were direct-bilateral strategies, such as talking, insinuating, interacting, and reasoning, while women reported using indirect-unilateral strategies such as threatening to cry, becoming silent, emotional blackmail, and doing things for themselves. These effects of gender differences were similar to the pattern found in terms of the effects of perceiving a balance of power in the relationship. People who perceived to have greater power than their partners were more likely to use direct-bilateral strategies. As for the models presented in this chapter, divergences and similarities are observed. In general, in the models developed in other countries, there is a great agreement between the strategies used to influence the behavior of the partner. However, the models that share the most strategies are the ones presented by French and Raven [8] and Parsons [35]. On the other hand, as for the models of Marwell and Schmitt [36] and Falbo and Peplau [37], it is observed that they find strategies that the previous models do not propose, such as threat, punishment, affection, altruism, persistence and offering (negotiation).

With respect to the strategies found in the mainstream literature compared to those observed in Mexico [38], many are compatible, especially with those proposed by Falbo and Peplau [37]; however, there are two strategies that had not been explicitly mentioned before, the sexual aspect, located within negative affect and authoritarianism and imposition (see **Table 2**).

3. Development of a power strategies measuring instrument for Mexico

This section is aimed at describing the process followed to develop a power strategies scale for Mexican couples. To this end, through the information obtained in the previous process, the items that represent the dimensions for each of the areas evaluated were created. The results of the previous steps made it possible to develop items to evaluate each of the areas of power strategies.

3.1 Participants

The instrument was developed based on the qualitative stage [51] and was applied to 748 subjects, 425 men and 323 women, with an age range between 17 and 66 years and an average of 29.15 years. As for marital status, 217 were single, 399 were married, and 127 were living in a common-law union. The median time in the relationship was 7.4 years living with their couple. The criteria for inclusion in the sample for those married and in a common-law union were: (a) that they lived together. This is in order to have daily coexistence. (b) Half with children and half without children, and (c) who had been married or living together for at least 1 year.

3.2 Instrument

Based on the definition given to each of the strategies found in the study by Rivera and Diaz-Loving [51], 149 statements were created on a Likert-type frequency scale (from never to always) that represents the two poles of strategies (positive and negative) used by men and women to exert influence or power over their couple.

3.3 Procedure

The questionnaire was applied to people who met the inclusion characteristics and who voluntarily wished to answer it. Research assistants went to different settings, such as private homes, schools, offices, clinics, and both private and state companies. The participants were asked to answer as truthfully as possible, assuring them that the information obtained would be confidential and that in no way would it affect the relationship with their partner or their personal life, that the data would be treated statistically for the population, and that no personal analysis would be carried out.

3.4 Psychometric analysis of the power strategies instrument

To evaluate the discriminating power of the items, the frequency distribution (bias and kurtosis) was analyzed, and a Student's t-test per item was also conducted. Next, the internal consistency of the total scale formed by the 130 items was obtained *via* a Cronbach's alpha, and a score of .9227 was obtained, indicating high congruence in the items evaluating each of the dimensions of power strategies.

Subsequently, a principal components factor analysis with an orthogonal rotation (varimax) was applied to obtain the dimensions and construct validity of the instrument. Fourteen factors with eigenvalues greater than 1 were found, which explains 50.3% of the variance. From this analysis, 130 items with a factor weight greater than or equal to .30 were chosen for each dimension (see **Table 3**). Only the first 12 items

Factor 1: AUTHORITARIANISM n = 21 α = .9060 μ = 63	**Factor weight**
I behave aggressively	.72061
I establish my will	.70896
I make her-him feel guilty even though he-she's right	.70848
I fake being annoyed	.68294
I control the money in the relationship	.63962
I criticize my partners behavior	.63728
I impose my conditions	.60418
I shout at my couple	.59798
I reprimand my couple	.53419
I raise my voice	. 53,419
Threaten to do things that will bother my couple	.47748
I impose my authority	.46979
Factor 2: POSITIVE AFFECT n = 18 α = .8867 μ = 54	
I hug my couple	.76771
I embrace and caress my couple	.74300
I am loving	.73430
I spoil my couple	.69973
I compliment my partner's qualities	.66642
I give my couple presents	.64802
I ask in the name of love	.64447

Factor 1: AUTHORITARIANISM n = 21 α = .9060 μ = 63	**Factor weight**
I run chores for my couple	.64235
I offer my unconditional love	.64158
I surprise my couple with a present	.64078
I smile	.58110
I am tender	.57982
Factor 3. EQUITY-RECIPROCITY n = 11 α = .8368 μ = 33	
I agree with my partner	.70404
I reach fair agreements through dialog	.68591
We come to agreements through dialog	.64586
I make my couple come to his-her senses by giving examples	.55667
I speak to my couple	.55061
I reason with my couple	.54633
I ask amicably	.47506
I ask politely	.47410
I explain the reason for my request	.45802
I look for mutual benefits	.43328
I take into account my partner's opinion	.42931
Factor 4: DIRECT-RATIONAL n = 11 α = .7584 μ = 33	
I justify my request under the rules	.78255
I am clear and direct	.74413
I make my partner see the advantages of what I ask	.70996
I make concise requests	.67043
I expose my reasons	.57532
I discuss my point of view	.54160
I suggest options	.51528
I analyze possible options	.51509
I negotiate with my partner	.49061
I am insistent	.41256
I am fair	.40654
Factor 5: IMPOSITION MANIPULATION n = 7 α = .6294 μ = 21	
I forbid my partner to say what they think	.77243
I discuss the pros and cons to convince my partner of my ways	−.76053
I repress my partner's interests	.70652
I remind my partner of the favors she-he still owes me	.68214
I present alternatives adequate for me	−.65123
I describe my partner's preferences as incorrect	.64220
I do not accept my partner's proposals	.42294
Factor 6: DISQUALIFY n = 6 α = .7829 μ = 18	
I disqualify my partner	.83622

Factor 1: AUTHORITARIANISM n = 21 α = .9060 μ = 63	**Factor weight**
I humiliate my partner	.76818
I state to my partner who brings the most money to the relationship	.63067
I usually prohibit activities of my partner	.50851
I ignore my couple	.50677
I make my partner believe that I accept their point of view	.49097
Factor 7: NEGATIVE AFFECT n = 12 α = .8097 μ = 36	
I deny my couple some material things	.76746
I emphasize my partner's flaws	.73093
I lie to my partner	.70708
I tell my partner I do not love her-him anymore	.65372
I make my partner jealous	.70708
I accuse my partner with people important to us	.68226
I punish my partner	.63885
I use the fear of punishment	.62347
I misguide my partner	.48383
I give excuses to my partner	.46118
I fake that I am sick	.45863
I avoid tell my partner that I love him-her	.45228
Factor 8: COERCION n = 5 α = .6453 μ = 15	
I use physical force	.78560
I use my physical attraction	.48362
I order my partner to obey me	.48298
I threaten my partner	.48034
I impose conditions on my partner	.46934
Factor 9: PASSIVE AGGRESSION n = 6 α = .7229 μ = 18	
I refuse to collaborate with my partner	.65229
I stop spoiling my partner	.58500
I do what I want without taking into account my partner's opinion	.57085
I am indifferent, as if nothing was happening	.53497
I reject my couple	.47555
I avoid the subject	.38231
Factor 10: BLACKMAIL n = 11 α = .7216 μ = 33	
I call myself incapable	.78274
I stop talking to my partner	.76015
I fake interest	.74041
I stop doing what my partner asks me to do	.73205
I pretend that I am sad	.72992
I cry	.64671
I try to frighten my partner	.63495

Factor 1: AUTHORITARIANISM n = 21 α = .9060 μ = 63	**Factor weight**
I play the martyr	.51406
I act as a defenseless being	.42498
I leave the scene	.38682
I fake physical incapability	.30776
Factor 11: AFFECT - PETITION n = 3 α = .6548 μ = 9	
I ask my partner to listen to me	.75642
I ask understanding from my couple	.54056
It ell my couple how important their support is to me	.46915
Factor 12: SELF-AFFIRMATION n = 5 α = .6808 μ = 15	
I take the final decision	.71261
I give direct orders	.57971
I give precise directions	.54959
I give something in return for obedience	.48786
I control my partner's activities	.35323
Factor 13: SEXUAL n = 7 α = .6925 μ = 21	
I sexually compliment my partner	.74052
I avoid sexual contact	.73789
I make love to my partner	.73076
I seduce my partner	.62141
I tell my partner that I do not want to have sex	.59814
I compliment my partner's physique	.48261
I make sexual innuendos	.45000
Factor 14: DOMINATION n = 6 α = .8013 μ = 18	
I remind my couple of the sacrifices I have made for him-her	.62582
I judge my partner severely	.42020
I provoke altercations to make partner bile	.68960
I behave rude	.64331
I question my partners authority in front of others	.56867
I behave violently	.46127

Table 3.
Factor analysis and internal consistency of the power strategies scales (ESPO).

with the highest weights will be presented in those cases where there are more than 12 items with weights over .30. It should be clarified that the factor analysis was applied separately for each sex; however, the result found for both groups was the same, since the factors appeared in the same order and with very similar factor weights.

The conceptual definitions of each factor and the strategy it represents appear in **Table 4**.

4. Correlation analysis between power strategies

Starting on the dark side of close relationships, as for the authoritarian factor, in general, it is observed that it is significantly related to all factors except for the two

Strategy	Definition	Indicators
Authoritarian	Participants use resources that show disapproval of their partner in response to the denials of what is desired.	Anger, faces, yelling, criticism, avoidance, demands, and nonsense
Positive affect	Participants address their partners with kind and affectionate behaviors to achieve their goals.	Love, gifts, recognition, cooperation, and affection
Equity-reciprocity	Participants offer an exchange to their partner in terms of mutually acceptable benefits, although they prioritize their interests.	Justice, tolerance, support, dialog, and exemplify
Direct-rational	Participants try to convince their partner to comply with their request using rational arguments.	Expose, suggest, analyze, explain, justify, and discuss
Imposition manipulation	Participants address their partner in a repressive and inflexible way in their attempt to influence the latter's criteria.	Prohibit, restrict, repress, and condemn
Disqualify	Participants act hostile and tyrannical toward their partner in response to their ungratified requests.	Harming, humiliating, and devaluing
Negative affect	Participants make use of painful and hurtful affective emotions that aim to hurt their partner when their requests are not fulfilled.	Punishment, use of fear, and taking away affection
Coercion	Participants use physical force and threats in an attempt to achieve their ends.	Forcing, ordering, threatening, and imposing
Passive aggression	Participants act contrary to what their partner values are, making partner feel disqualified or non-existent.	Not collaborating, indifferent, and rejecting
Blackmail	When trying to convince their partner, participants make use of justifications that aim to make their partner feel responsible and even guilty.	Incapacitated, helpless, fearful, and sad
Kind petition	Participants act in a respectful and flattering manner with their partner so that they attend to their requests.	Understanding, sharing status, attention, and support
Self-affirmative	Participants enunciate their requests openly, with the certainty of an implicit or explicit existing duty.	Direct, decisive, and informative
Sexual	Participant withdraws sexual and emotional affection in response to the non-gratification of their request.	Avoidance of sexual approach
Dominion	Participants behave punitively and very directly about what they have identified as annoying in their partner.	Unfriendly, disqualifying, violating

Table 4.
Definitions of strategies and their indicators.

factors that have to do with affect (positive affect and affect-request), with which there is no relationship. On the other hand, the greater the authoritarianism, the less equity and reciprocity in the relationship ($r = -.36$; $p = .01$); this implies that when the couple behaves aggressively, angry, and controlling, they do not reach agreements or dialog. Regarding the positive correlations, the greater the authoritarianism, the greater the coercion ($r = .62$; $p = .01$), the passive aggression ($r = .61$, $p = .01$), dominance ($r = .60$; $p = .01$), self-affirmation ($r = .59$; $p = .01$), imposition manipulation ($r = .58$; $p = .01$), negative affect ($r = .52$; $p = .01$), blackmail ($r = .50$; $p = .01$), and number of negative sexual behaviors ($r = -.30$; $p = .01$). In general, the partner who is more aggressive, angry and controlling, is also more threatening, imposing, does not collaborate, is indifferent, judges severely, gives direct orders, is prohibitive and repressive, mentions the partner who does not love her, cries and is defenseless, avoiding sexual approaches.

The very negative factor on disqualifying the partner is positively and significantly related to negative affect ($r = .38$; $p = .01$), coercion ($r = .37$; $p = .01$), dominance ($r = .36$; $p = .01$), blackmail ($r = -.30$; $p = .01$), and imposition manipulation ($r = -.28$; $p = .01$). It also correlates negatively and significantly with request affect ($r = -.13$; $p = .01$). When a member of a couple humiliates and prohibits their partner, they also lie to them, indicating they do not love them, using physical force, ordering, crying, and showing sadness, as well as repressing and condemning the couple's proposals. Something similar occurs with the dominating strategy that shows positive and significant correlations with all negative factors, including coercion ($r = .51$; $p = .01$), negative affection ($r = .47$; $p = .01$), passive aggression ($r = .44$; $p = .01$), blackmail ($r = .42$; $p = .01$), imposition manipulation ($r = .31$; $p = .01$), and the negative aspect of the sexual part ($r = .44$; $p = .01$). Continuing on the dark side of relationships, negative affect strategy shows positive and significant correlations with: coercion ($r = .48$; $p = .01$), blackmail ($r = .47$; $p = .01$), passive aggression ($r = .43$; $p = .01$), self-affirmation ($r = .38$; $p = .01$), imposition manipulation ($r = .33$; $p = .01$) and the sexual aspect ($r = .23$; $p = .01$).

With reference to the use of sexual encounters as a strategy to control their partner, positive and significant correlations are found with three factors: passive aggression ($r = .38$; $p = .01$), blackmail ($r = .28$; $p = .01$) and coercion ($r = .22$; $p = .01$). The partner who denies sexual intercourse to the partner also tends not to collaborate, to be indifferent, to cry, to be sad, to stop talking, to use physical force, to order and to threaten. An alternative form of negative control is found in the passive-aggressive strategy. That is when the subject is indifferent and refuses to collaborate. This strategy shows positive and significant correlations with blackmail ($r = .51$; $p = .01$), coercion ($r = .44$; $p = .01$), and imposition of manipulation ($r = .38$; $p = .01$). These correlations show that the subject in the face of this strategy is sad, cries, uses physical force and threats, as well as prohibits and represses the decisions of the partner. As a corollary to the dark side, coercion is positively and significantly associated with blackmail ($R = .41$; $p = .01$) and imposition of manipulation ($r = .37$; $p = .01$). In other words, participants use physical force, orders, and threats, and then if that does not work, they also cry and say that they are sad, ending with forbidding the partner of saying what they think.

On the lighter side of close relationships, there is a conglomerate of strategies being used. For the positive affect strategy, positive and significant correlations are observed with the equity-reciprocity strategies ($r = .50$; $p = .01$) and request affect ($r=. 52$; $p = .01$). When one of the members of the couple is perceived as cuddly, loving and flattering, the couple reaches more agreements, dialog and asks for support and understanding from the other member. Within this same factor, the highest negative correlation was with the strategy called passive aggression ($r = -.20$; $p = .01$), where the subject who perceives himself as more loving and affective when asking their partner for something would make less use of a strategy of not collaborating, being indifferent and judging their partner severely. Other strategies that correlate negatively and significantly with positive affect are being less disqualifying ($r = -.10$; $p = .05$), less manipulative in the sexual aspect ($r = -.12$; $p = .01$), less dominant ($r = -.09$; $p = .05$), coercive ($r = -.08$; $p = .05$), and imposing and manipulative ($r = -.09$; $p = .05$).

In this regard, the equity-reciprocity strategy, more common in horizontal collectivistic cultures [46], when there are agreements and dialog in the couple, there is greater affection-request ($r = .44$; $p = .01$). Equity also leads to being direct and rational, the more the couple talks and dialogs, the more they give rational reasons and talk about the advantages of the requests. As to negative and significant correlations for this factor, this strategy is negatively related to passive aggression ($r = -.41$; $p = .01$), negative affect ($r = -.12$; $p = .01$), disqualifying ($r = -.33$; $p = .01$), dominance ($r = -.31$; $p = .01$), blackmail ($r = -.31$; $p = .01$), coercion ($r = -.32$; $p = .01$), and the negative part of sexuality ($r = -.22$; $p = .01$).

Congruent with a Mexican culture that is more inclined to use indirect methods to express needs and likes [52], self-affirmation and direct communications can be seen as not as polite. This can explain why the rational direct factor has positive and significant correlations with the dimensions of imposition, manipulation ($r = .50$; $p = .01$), affect, request ($r = .34$; $p = .01$), and self-affirmation ($r = .22$; $p = .01$). Within the area of self-affirmation, positive correlations are found with the strategies of coercion ($r = .49$; $p = .01$), imposition, manipulation ($r = .42$; $p = .01$), and passive aggression ($r = .31$; $p = .01$). Under these findings, it is found that people who give direct orders and precise indications, make use of other strategies linked to physical force, imposition and threat, as well as situations related to prohibiting and repressing and being rejecting and indifferent to the partner.

5. Confirmatory factor analysis

In order to insure structural validity for the new strategies instrument, it was administered to a sample of 672 people, 320 men and 352 women, with an age range of 18 to 72 years ($M = 32.79$, $SD = 10.4$). About 84.2% were married, 12.3% were in a common-law union and 3.3% were single. 83.3% had children and 16.7% did not.

Confirmatory Factor Analysis (CFA), Structural Equation Models (SEM; [53]). Following the proposal of Shi and Maydeu-Olivares [54], and based on the ordinal nature of the items, it was decided to use the diagonally weighted least squares (DWLS) method for the estimation of the model. The fit of the model was assessed using the indicators recommended by Hu and Bentler [55], that is, comparative fit index (CFI), Tucker-Lewis index (TLI), square root of measurement residuals (SRMR), and approximate mean square error (RMSEA). While the interpretation of these was made following the proposal of Marsh et al. [56], that is, CFI and TLI values $\geq .90$ and RMSEA and SRMR $\leq .08$ reflect an acceptable fit.

6. Results

Once estimated, the model presents adequate goodness-of-fit indicators [χ^2 (1774) = 3295.190, $p \leq .001$; CFI = 0.945, TLI = 0.941, RMSEA = .042 [90% IC .040–.044] and SRMR = 0.067]. **Figure 1** presents the diagram of this model and presents the covariances between the closest factors, while **Table 5** presents all the covariances. The final inventory of power strategies is presented at the end of this chapter.

DOI: http://dx.doi.org/10.5772/intechopen.1010251

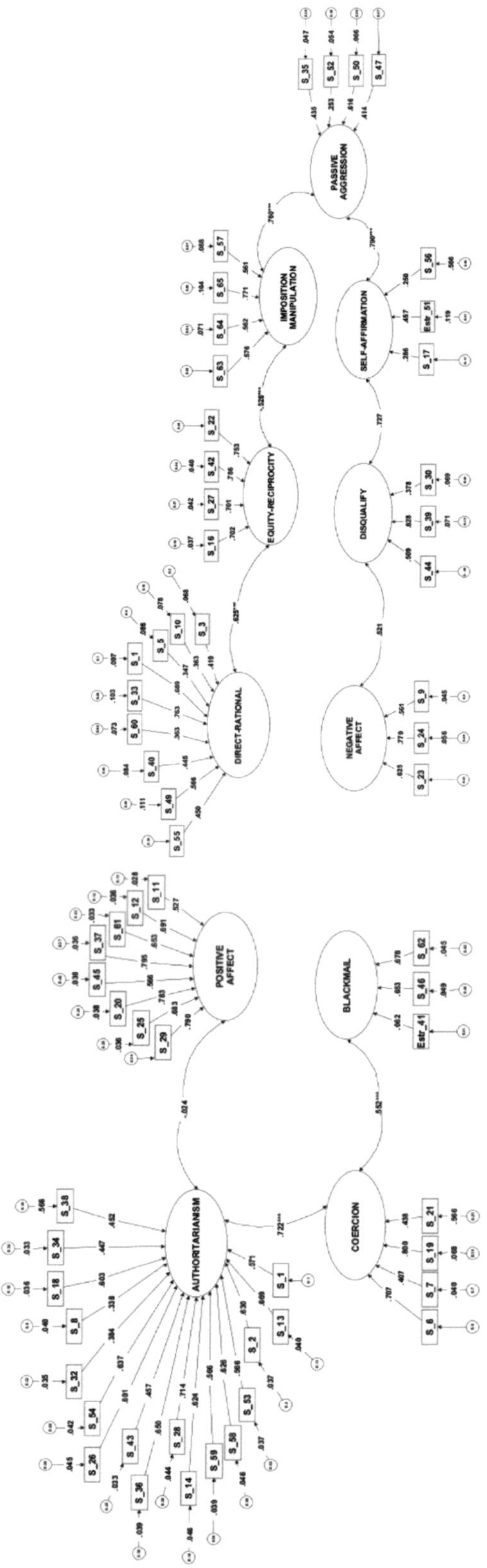

Figure 1.
Confirmatory model of the Power Strategies scale. *$p < .05$, **$p > .01$, ***$p > .001$.

	1	2	3	4	5	6	7	8	9	10	11
1	—										
2	−.024*	—									
3	−.216***	.197***	—								
4	−.543***	.447***	.625***	—							
5	.734***	−.104***	−.283***	−.526***	—						
6	.722***	.059**	−.184***	−.403***	.583***	—					
7	.788***	−.080***	−.143***	−.487***	.804***	.552***	—				
8	.677***	−.099***	−.141***	−.472***	.534***	.570***	.481***	—			
9	.772***	−.128***	−.297***	.589***	.693***	.702***	.752***	.521***	—		
10	.966***	.362***	.229***	−.341***	.770***	.906***	.925***	.568***	.727***	—	
11	.840***	−.052*	−.209***	−.518***	.760***	.550***	.663***	.566***	.754***	.790***	—

1. Authoritarian; 2. Sexual Positive affect; 3. Direct-rational; 4. Equity-reciprocity; 5. Imposition manipulation; 6. Coercion; 7. Blackmail; 8. Negative Sexual; 9. Disqualify; 10, Self-affirmative; 11. Passive aggression. $^{*}p < .05$.
$^{**}p > .01$.
$^{***}p > .001$.

Table 5.
Covariance matrix between power strategies factors.

7. Conclusions

From the perspective of the mainstream, sound measures must demonstrate content validity, criterion-related validity, construct validity, and internal consistency [57]. These criteria determine the psychometric validation of behavioral measures. We would argue that cultural validity is not a distinct type of validity; rather, it underpins the entire concept of validity. Thus, each time a construct and its measurement are developed, the ways in which language and culture form a part of the validity argument must be considered [58]. On the other hand, if cultural validity issues are addressed properly at the inception of an assessment, there would be no cultural bias [59]. Thus, the cultural relevance and sensitivity of psychometric measures is central to the appropriate use and comparison within and across cultures, which is stressed in the attention paid to the equivalence and reduction of bias of meaning and measurement discussed in the cross-cultural literature [6, 60, 61].

Indigenous psychology in different cultures allows the evaluation of universal and idiosyncratic theories of human behavior. Autochthonous researchers are particularly aware of the impact of social, ecological, and cultural variables on the acquisition, development, dynamics, and establishment of psychological consistencies. This consciousness centers their attention on culture, which provides the theoretical framework for explaining how groups of individuals arrive at shared yet distinctive sets of values, attributes, attitudes, and behaviors [62]. On the one hand, this allows for the discovery of seemingly idiosyncratic characteristics, which are non-existent in other cultures or at least not present in their psychological literature. Vernacular psychologies also permit an in-depth study of relations and causality of sets of culturally relevant variables and their relation to those of the "mainstream" and its universal constructs [6].

Appendix

Power strategies inventory

Table A1, you will find a series of behaviors that describe the way in which one member of a couple acts to convince their partner to do or say what they want, please indicate what you do to influence your partner, by answering the following statement:

"When trying to get my partner to do something that I want..."

1. Never 2. Seldom 3. Sometimes 4. Frequently 5. Always

I reprimand my partner
I make my partner see the advantages of what I ask of him or her
I take into account my partner's opinion
I threaten my partner
I offer alternatives
I discuss the pros and cons of my petition
I control my partner's activities
I show my discontent
I take money away
I ask directly
I smile
I order obedience
I use physical force
I use affectionate diminutives
I play the martyr
I am affectionate
I make him or her feel guilty even if he or she is right
I insist
I tell my partner that I do not want to have sex
I make clear-cut requests
I offer gifts
I praise his or her qualities
I behave aggressively
I pretend to be angry
I negotiate
I control the money of the relationship
I converse with my partner
I hug and caress him or her
I pretend to be sad
I refuse to collaborate with my partner
I offer him or her my unconditional love
I impose my will
I criticize his or her behavior
I cuddle my partner
I move away from my partner
I agree with my partner
I stop consenting to their wishes
I am indifferent, as if nothing was happening
I offer options

I reprimand my partner
I avoid sexual closeness
I reject my partner
I make love to my partner
I do what I want without taking into account his or hers opinion
I reach fair agreements through dialog
I impose conditions on my partner
I act like a helpless being
I Sexually compliment my partner
I fake being injured or hurt
I do some of my partner's chores
I present pleasant aspects of myself
I feign interest in him (her)
I participate in my partner's activities
I justify my request under the rules
I threaten to do things that will bother my partner
I cry
I try to scare my partner
I explain the logic behind of my request
I cordially ask
I make my partner feel jealous
I call myself incapable
I kindly ask
I compliment my partner's physique
I explain the reason for my request
I make suggestions
I stop speaking to my partner
I ignore my partner
I ask for shares support
I avoid tell my partner I love him or her
I'm fair to my partner
I am loving
I usually prohibit activities from my partner
I humiliate my partner
I ask my partner for understanding
I tell my partner who brings the most money to the relationship
I ask in the name of the love you have for me
I often lie to my partner
I do harm to my partner

I reprimand my partner
I talk to my partner
I avoid the topic (I pretend I do not listen)
I make my partner believe that I accept their point of view
I spoil my partner
I use bad words
I make the final decision
I remind my partner of the sacrifices I have made for him (her)
I shout at my partner
I stop doing what my partner asks me to do
I bargain looking for my own advantage
I surprise my partner with gifts or surprises
I use deceitfulness
I enforce y authority
I use my physical attractiveness
I claim things from the past
I argue in favor of my point of view
I demand that my partner honors our agreements
I talk about the importance of his-her support
I tell my partner that I do not love him-her anymore
I use the fear of punishment
I punish my partner
I give direct orders
I raise my voice
I give something in return
I behave negatively
I disqualify my partners authority in the eyes of others
I behave violently
I fake illness
I try to get on my partners good side
I ask my partner to listen to me
I give straightforward instructions
I offer gifts
I try to reason with my partner
I deny my partner some material things
I am inaccessible to any proposals
I judge my partner harshly
I provoke altercations to make my partner bitter
I accuse my partner with people important to us
I make my partner come to his-her senses, by giving examples

I reprimand my partner
I recognize my partners abilities in public
I seduce my partner
I analyze viable options
I emphasize my partners flaws
I forbid my partner to say what he or she thinks
I condemn my partners decisions as incorrect
I limit my partners initiatives
I remind my partner of the favors she or he still owes me

Table A1.
Power strategies scale for Mexican couples (PSSMC).

Author details

Rolando Diaz-Loving*, Sofia Rivera Aragon
and Marcoantonio Villanueva Bustamante
National Autonomous University of Mexico, Mexico

*Address all correspondence to: rdiazl@unam.mx

References

[1] Díaz-Guerrero R. El problema de la definición operante de la identidad nacional mexicana. [The problema with the oerational definition of the Mexican national identity]. Revista Mexicana de Psicología. 1986;**3**:109-119

[2] Díaz-Guerrro R. Towards an ecosystemic psychology. In: Keats JA, Taft R, Heath RA, Lovibond SH, editors. Mathematical and Theoretical Systems. Amsterdam: North-Holland; 1989. pp. 229-240

[3] Díaz-Guerrro. Abnegación, un Factor Cardinal en la Personalidad de los mexicanos. [Abenegation, a cardinal factor of Mexican personality]. Revista de Psicología Social y Personalidad. 1993;**9**(2):1-19

[4] Díaz-Guerrero R. Crónica de la premisa histórico-socio-cultural (P.H.S.C.). [Chronicle of the psico-socio-cultural premises]. In: Díaz-Guerrero R, Pacheco AM, editors. Etnopsicología: Scientia Nova. San Juan, Puerto Rico: Servicios Profesionales y Científicos, Inc.; 1994. pp. 41-60

[5] Díaz-Guerrero R. Origins and development of Mexican ethnopsychology. World Psychology. 1995;**1**:49-68

[6] Diaz-Loving R. Ethno-Psychometry: The measurement of personality in Mexico. Online Readings in Psychology and Culture. 2025;**3**(1):1-20. DOI: 10.9707/2307-0919.1206

[7] Rivera AS, Díaz Loving R. Significado y Distribución del Poder en la Pareja. [Meaning and distribution of power in couples]. Revista de Psicología Social y Personalidad. 1995;**XI**(2):159-172

[8] French J Jr, Raven B. The bases of social power. In: Cartwright D, editor. Studies in Social Power. Ann Arbor: University of Michigan Press; 1959. pp. 150-163

[9] Kipnis D. The use of power in organizations and in interpersonal settings. In: Oskamp S, editor. (De). Applied Social Psychology Annual. Vol. 5. Beverly Hills, CA: SAGE; 1984. pp. 179-210

[10] Thibaut JW, Kelley HH. The Social Psychology of Groups. New York: Wiley; 1959

[11] Cartwright D, Alvin Z. A field theoretical conception of power. In: Cartwright D, editor. Studies in Social Power. Ann Arbr: University of Michigan; 1959. pp. 183-220

[12] Homans GC. Social Behaviour: Its Elementary Forms. New York: Harcourt, Brace and World; 1961

[13] Etizioni A. A Comparative Analysis of Couples Organizations. New York: Macmillan; 1961

[14] Rodman. Marital power and the theory of resources in cultural context. Journal Comparative Family Studies: Spr. 1972;**3**:60-69

[15] Safilios-Rothschild C. 1970,The study of family power structure: A review, 1960-1969. Journal of Marriage and the Family. 1976;**32**:539-552

[16] Kenneth GJ. The Anatomy of Power. Boston: Houghton Mifflin; 1983

[17] Lewin K. Field Theory in the Social Science. New York: Harper and Row; 1985

[18] Boulding KE. Las tres caras del poder. México: Paidos; 1994

[19] Corrales RG. Power and satisfaction in early marriage. In: Cromwell RE, Olson DH, editors. Power in Families. New York: Wiley; 1975

[20] Gray, Little B. Marital quality and power processes among black couples. Journal of Marriage and the Family. 1982;**44**:633-646

[21] Olson DH, Rabunsky C. Validity of four measures of family power. Journal of Marriage and the Family. 1972;**34**:224-234

[22] Olson DH. The measurement of family power by self-report and behavioural methods. Journal of Marriage and the Family. 1969;**31**:545-550

[23] Turk JL, Bell NW. Measuring power in families. Journal of Marriage and the Family. 1972;**34**:215-222

[24] Cromwell RE, Klein DM, Wieting SG. Family power: A multitrait-multimethod analysis. In: Cromwell RE, Olson DH, editors. Power in Families. New York: Wiley; 1975

[25] Olson DH, Cromwell RE. Power in families. In: Cromwell RE, Olson DH, editors. Power in Families. New York: John, Wiley, and Sons; 1975. pp. 3-37

[26] Jacob T. Family interaction in disturbed and normal families: A methodological and substantive review. Psychological Bulletin. 1975;**82**:33-65

[27] Cowan G, Drinkard J, McGavin L. The effects of target, age and gender on use of power strategies. Journal of Personality and Social Psychology. 1984;**47**:1391-1398

[28] Blood RO, Wolfe DM. Husbands and Wives: The Dynamics of Married Living. Glencoe, IL: The Free Press; 1969

[29] Lu YC. Marital roles and marriage adjustment. Sociology and Social Research. 1952;**36**:364-368

[30] Centers R, Raven BH, Rodrigues A. Conjugal power structure: A re-examination. American Sociological Review. 1971;**36**:264-278

[31] Sargent H. Intrapsychic change: Methodological problems in psychotherapy research. Psychiatry. 1961;**24**:93-108

[32] Gray, Little B, Burks N. Power and satisfaction in marriage: A review and critique. Psychological Bulletin. 1983;**93**(3):513-538

[33] Raven BH, Centers R, Rodrigues A. The bases of conjugal power. In: Cromwell RE, Olson DH, editors. Power in Families. New York: Academic Press; 1975. pp. 217-232

[34] Kelman HC. Processes of opinion change. Public Opinion Quarterly. 1961;**25**:57-78

[35] Parsons T. On the concept of influence. Public Opinion Quarterly. 1963;**27**:37-62

[36] Marwell G, Schmitt DR. Dimensions of compliance- gaining behavior: An empirical analysis. Sociometry. 1967;**30**:350-364

[37] Falbo T, Peplau LA. Power strategies in intimate relationships. Journal of Personality and Social Psychology. 1980;**38**:618-628

[38] Rivera AS, Díaz Loving R, Sánchez AR, Alvarado HVI. Estilos y estrategias del poder en la Pareja: Un estudio exploratorio. [Power styles and strategies in couples: An exploratory study]. La Psicología Social en México. 1996;**VI**:310-315. Ed. AMEPSO

[39] Reyes LI. Las Redes Semánticas Naturales, su conceptualización y su utilización en la construcción de instrumentos. [Natural semantic networks, their conceptualization and use in development of measuring instruments]. Revista de Psicología Social y Personalidad. 1993;**9**(1):81-97

[40] Krippendorff K. Metodología de análisis de contenido: teoría y práctica. Barcelona: Paidós; 1990

[41] Bacharach SB, Lawler E. Bargaining, Power, Tactics and Outcome. San Francisco: Jossey Bass; 1981

[42] Blalock HM Jr, Wilken PH. Intergroup Processes: A Micro-Macro Perspective. New York: The Free Press; 1979

[43] Scanzoni J. Social exchange and behavioral interdependence. In: Burgess RL, Huston TL, editors. Contemporary Theories about the Family: Research-Based Theories. Vol. 1. New York: Academic Press; 1979. pp. 295-316

[44] Sprey J. Family power and process: Toward a conceptual integration. In: Cromwell RE, Olson DH, editors. Power in Families. New York: John, Wiley and Sons; 1975. pp. 61-79

[45] Wrong DH. Power: Its Forms, Bases and Uses. New York: Harper and Row; 1979

[46] Triandis HC. Cultura: El nuevo énfasis en Psicología. Revista de Psicología Social y Personalidad. X. 1994;**1**:1-17

[47] Díaz Guerrero R, Díaz Loving R. El amor y el poder en México. La Psicología Social en México. 1988;**II**:153-159 [Love and power in Mexico]

[48] Bird GW, Bird GA, Scruggs M. Determinants of family task sharing: A study of husbands and wives. Journal of Marriage and the Family. 1984;**46**(2):345-355

[49] Lee GR, Pertersen LR. Conjugal power and spousal resources in patriarchal cultures. Journal of Comparative Family Studies. 1983;**14**:23-38

[50] Warner RL, Lee GR, Lee J. Social organization, spousal resources and marital power: A cross-cultural study. Journal of Marriage and the Family. 1986;**48**:121-128

[51] Rivera AS, Díaz Loving R. Estrategias de Poder en la Relación de Pareja. [Power strategies in couple relationships]. In: Diaz Loving R, editor. Antología Psicosocial de la Pareja. México: Porrúa; 1999. pp. 183-214

[52] Flores Galaz MM, Diaz-Loving R. Escala multidimensional de asertividad. México: Manual Moderno; 2004

[53] Kline RB. Principles and Practice of Structural Equation Modeling. 4th ed. Guilford Press; 2016

[54] Shi D, Maydeu-Olivares A. The effect of estimation methods on SEM fit indices. Educational and Psychological Measurement. 2020;**80**(3):421-445. DOI: 10.1177/0013164419885164

[55] Hu LT, Bentler PM. Cutoff criteria for fit indexes in covariance structure analysis: Conventional criteria versus new alternatives. Structural Equation Modeling. 1999;**6**:1-55. DOI: 10.1080/10705519909540118

[56] Marsh HW, Hau KT, Wen Z. In search of golden rules: Comment on hypothesis-testing approaches to setting cutoff values for fit indexes and

dangers in overgeneralizing Hu and Bentler's (1999) findings. Structural Equation Modeling. 2004;**11**(3):320-341. DOI: 10.1207/s15328007sem1103_2

[57] Jhangiani R, S, Chant I, Chiang A, Cuttler C, Leighton DC. Research Methods in Psychology. 4th ed. Minneapolis, MN, USA: KPU Open Publishing; 2024. Available from: http://bit.ly/203_textbook. ISBN: 978-1-9991981-0-7

[58] Solano-Flores G. Assessing the cultural validity of assessment practices: An introduction. In: Basterra MDR, Trumbull E, Solano-Flores G, editors. Cultural Validity in Assessment: Addressing Linguistic and Cultural Diversity. London, UK: Routledge; 2011. pp. 3-21

[59] Solano-Flores G, Nelson-Barber S. On the cultural validity of science assessments. Journal of Research in Science Teaching. 2001;**38**(5):553-573

[60] He J, van de Vijver F. Bias and equivalence in cross-cultural research. Online Readings in Psychology and Culture. 2012;**2**(2). DOI: 10.9707/2307-0919.1111

[61] Padilla AM, Borsato GN. Issues in culturally appropriate psychoeducational assessment. In: Suzuki LA, Ponterotto JG, editors. Handbook of Multicultural Assessment: Clinical, Psychological, and Educational Applications. New Jersey, USA: Jossey-Bass/Wiley; 2008. pp. 5-21

[62] Díaz-Loving R. Ethnopsychology: Pieces from the Mexican Research Gallery. Springer Nature; 2019. pp. 1-186

Chapter 4

Deep Learning Applications for Analysis of Unstructured Data

Zekai Wei, Yilei Wang and Deniz S. Ones

Abstract

This study investigated the use of deep learning to automate the classification of environmental initiatives in organizational research. We focused on transformer-based models, including BERT and large language models (LLMs), as scalable alternatives to traditional content analysis methods. Two experiments were conducted: the first compared deep learning models with conventional machine learning approaches, while the second evaluated the performance of various LLM prompting configurations. BERT outperformed traditional models, achieving a weighted F1-score of 0.74, while fine-tuned GPT-3.5-turbo surpassed all models with an F1-score of 0.77. In contrast, base versions of GPT models underperformed relative to simpler classifiers. These findings underscored the benefits of fine-tuning for domain-specific tasks and demonstrated that deep learning models can automate text classification without manual feature engineering. The study also identified challenges, including lower performance in rare categories and hallucination issues in some LLM configurations. Overall, this research advanced methodological practices in psychological and organizational science by showcasing how deep learning can strengthen computer-aided content analysis. The results further pointed to the value of hybrid approaches that combine automated methods with expert validation to improve reliability.

Keywords: deep learning, large language models, LLMs, organizational sustainability, content analysis, organizational environmental initiatives

1. Introduction

Over recent decades, machine learning (ML) and natural language processing (NLP) have been increasingly integrated into social and behavioral science research practice to analyze unstructured data. Computer-aided content analysis (CACA) exemplifies this trend, offering a more efficient and scalable alternative to traditional content analysis, which is often labor-intensive, costly, and dependent on input from subject matter experts (SMEs). Early CACA techniques primarily relied on word frequency analysis, using predefined content dictionaries to identify text topics [1, 2]. As NLP techniques became more advanced and accessible, Pollach [3] advocated for the integration of corpus linguistics, a methodology foundational to both linguistics and NLP, into content analysis, promoting its use in computer-aided approaches.

More recently, researchers have increasingly adopted NLP-driven approaches for content analysis tasks such as sentiment analysis, text classification, and discourse analysis [4, 5]. This progression has enabled the analysis of increasingly complex unstructured datasets, allowing for deeper insights into social and behavioral phenomena all the while maintaining scalability and efficiency.

While recent advances in NLP have expanded the capabilities of CACA, particularly for complex tasks like sentiment analysis and discourse classification, these systems remain constrained by key limitations when built on shallow machine learning models. First, they still require feature engineering, a process that relies on researchers to manually extract meaningful features from text before applying machine learning algorithms [4]. This dependence on human intervention not only increases the time and labor costs but also introduces potential biases in feature selection. Second, CACA often fails to achieve satisfactory results when analyzing texts that are highly contextual or nuanced, as traditional ML models struggle to capture deep semantic meanings, contextual relationships, and domain-specific language. As a result, researchers have explored hybrid approaches that incorporate human expertise to refine computer-generated outputs, balancing computational efficiency with the need for accurate and context-aware analysis. However, this hybrid approach further increases the time and effort required from researchers, ultimately undermining the original objective of CACA—to provide a more efficient and scalable alternative to traditional approaches.

In response, researchers are adopting models that eliminate the need for manual feature engineering while capturing deeper, context-sensitive patterns in language. One advanced ML technique that remains comparatively underutilized in psychological research is deep learning. It is consistent with the emergence of a new generation of NLP methods—scalable, automated, and capable of more nuanced content analysis. Unlike traditional ML models trained on hand-constructed features, deep learning uses multi-layer neural networks to automatically construct hierarchical feature representations, enabling a deeper and more task-relevant understanding of data [6, 7]. In natural language processing (NLP), deep learning eliminates the need for manual feature engineering by allowing models to learn semantic representations at multiple levels—ranging from individual words and phrases to entire documents. Furthermore, deep learning enables the integration of domain knowledge directly into network design by encoding prior knowledge into the architecture itself or through specialized training strategies [8].

The slow and limited adoption of deep learning in psychology is likely due to the complexity of neural network models, which require substantial technical expertise in computer science alongside domain-specific knowledge. Furthermore, these models tend to sacrifice transparency and interpretability for predictive accuracy, complicating their use in fields that value explanatory insight [9, 10]. Recent developments in Large Language Models (LLMs), particularly transformer-based models like Generative Pre-trained Transformer (GPT), have made NLP tools more accessible to researchers, reducing the need for extensive coding expertise. However, despite their growing popularity, the reliability and validity of LLMs for computer-aided content analysis (CACA) need further examination.

This paper describes and advocates for the broader integration of deep learning techniques in psychological research. Using a case study, we examine a practical challenge faced by organizational psychology researchers and demonstrate the potential of neural networks and Large Language Models (LLMs) in CACA through two experiments. The manuscript first outlines the research problem, then details the methodology and findings, and concludes with a discussion of the results and their implications.

1.1 Background and overview of the research problem

Climate change and environmental sustainability are global challenges which modern organizations aim to address through their mitigation and adaptation initiatives [11]. To assess and enhance these efforts, organizations and researchers must systematically capture and classify the actions companies take. Accurate categorization of environmental initiatives provides a starting point for measuring, understanding, explaining, predicting, and changing organization's efforts toward environmental sustainability [12]. This process enables companies and society to assess corporate sustainability efforts, supports benchmarking across organizations, and promotes collective action on environmental challenges. Traditionally, content analysis of environmental initiatives has relied on manual coding by subject matter experts (SMEs), who classify initiatives based on predefined coding schemes. However, for researchers studying organizational environmental initiatives across large samples of organizations or extended time periods, the need to categorize tens of thousands of initiatives renders manual coding impractical. Moreover, manual classification is prone to clerical errors, coder fatigue, and subjectivity, raising concerns about consistency and validity.

The limitations of manual coding underscore the need for a fast, reliable, and automated classification system that minimizes human intervention. From a scientific perspective, automating the classification of environmental initiatives enables researchers to conduct large-scale empirical studies with improved replicability, transparency, and methodological rigor. Automated systems can handle vast volumes of data quickly and consistently, making it possible to track trends, evaluate policy impacts, and generate insights at a scale that would be infeasible with manual methods alone. From a practical standpoint, automated classification supports real-time monitoring and decision-making for sustainability practitioners and policymakers. It allows organizations to evaluate their initiatives more efficiently, compare them against industry benchmarks, and identify gaps or opportunities in their sustainability strategies. Furthermore, it enhances the capacity of regulatory bodies, NGOs, and other stakeholders to assess environmental performance and hold companies accountable. In response, organizational psychology scholars have begun exploring machine learning as a potential solution for automating this process. For example, Wang et al. [5] examined the use of traditional machine learning techniques for classifying environmental initiatives. Building on this foundation, this paper presents two experiments applying neural networks and large language models (LLMs) to the classification of organizational environmental initiatives. In the first experiment, we employed neural networks to categorize environmental initiatives and compared their performance to traditional machine learning models reported by Wang et al. [5]. By evaluating model performance on the same task, we can examine whether the additional complexity and computational demands of deep models yield substantial improvements in classification accuracy. In the second experiment, we used LLMs to classify environmental initiatives, comparing the performance of nine model configurations that varied by base model and prompting techniques. These comparisons help researchers optimize model selection and configuration for psychological research contexts.

2. Experiment 1

2.1 Methods

2.1.1 Dataset

The dataset for this study was obtained from a research project examining the environmental initiatives of large business organizations in China, Germany, France, the United Kingdom, and the Middle East and North Africa (MENA) region based on their self-reported sustainability efforts in publicly available reports. The dataset included 9795 environmental initiatives and their associated environmental impacts, collected from 326 organizations through Corporate Social Responsibility (CSR) reports published in 2015 and 2016 [13–15]. Each initiative was categorized according to a pre-validated, action- and behavior-focused taxonomy of organizational environmental sustainability initiatives [16, 17]. This taxonomy builds upon the employee green behaviors framework by Ones and Dilchert [17, 18] and extends it to the organizational level. It consists of 16 categories, each representing a distinct behavioral pathway for achieving environmental sustainability, which are further grouped under five overarching content-based themes. Definitions and illustrative examples of these categories are presented in **Table 1**. To ensure consistent classification, two trained human coders independently assigned each initiative to one of the 16 categories based on both the initiative itself and its reported consequences. In cases where discrepancies arose between the two coders, a third independent coder was consulted, and the majority decision was adopted. When consensus was not achieved, the classification was finalized through discussion.

2.1.2 Data preprocessing

Unlike traditional machine learning methods that require extensive data cleaning and normalization, deep learning models demand minimal preprocessing. In this study, we partitioned the dataset into training (80%), validation (10%), and test (10%) sets. The training set facilitates model learning, the validation set monitors performance during training, and the test set provides an independent evaluation of the final model. For text preprocessing, we used TensorFlow's Keras tools to break down the text into individual tokens (such as words or phrases), which were then automatically transformed into word embeddings that are numerical representations that deep learning models use to capture the meaning and relationships between words.

2.1.3 Model training

We chose two deep learning models, Recurrent Neural Network (RNN) and Bidirectional Encoder Representation from Transformers (BERT) because of their ability to capture complex language patterns and context in text data. Details about model architecture and configuration of RNN and BERT are presented in **Figures A1** and **A2**. Both models were trained on the identical training-validation-test split to ensure comparability of the results. During training, both models use softmax as their activation function for the final layer, which is commonly used for multi-class classification. Softmax function converts the values into probabilities, where the result of each value is proportional to the exponentials of the original values. Therefore, the resulting values amplify the differences in the input, and serve as the likelihood of the input belonging to each class. Both models then use categorical cross entropy,

Category of Initiative/ Behaviors covered	Description/example
Transforming	**Initiatives that change business products and processes to be more sustainable or use innovation to develop new more sustainable solutions**
Creating sustainable products and processes	Design and build ships powered by liquid natural gas (LNG)
Embracing innovation for sustainability	Adopt modern comprehensive mechanized mining technology
Choosing responsible alternatives	Insist on the procurement of environmentally certified office equipment
Changing how work is done	Rationalize construction schedules to reduce energy consumption
Avoiding harm	**Initiatives that avoid, mitigate or restore negative environmental impacts**
Monitoring environmental impact	Carry out carbon emission reporting
Preventing pollution	Complete Atmospheric VOC emissions special remediation
Strengthening ecosystems	Conduct bird activity monitoring
Conserving	**Initiatives that control (e.g., limit, reduce) resource use**
Reducing use	Require double-sided printing
Reusing	Reuse old office equipment
Repurposing	Use fly ash to produce light insulation bricks
Recycling	Develop a waste sorting program to sort waste with reuse value at the source
Influencing others	**Initiatives that provide information, skill, or motivation for others to perform sustainable actions**
Encouraging and supporting others	Encourage employees to take public transport to and from work and reduce self-driving
Educating and training for sustainability	Organized three special training sessions on energy saving and auction reduction awareness
Taking initiative	**Initiatives that proactively initiate broader organizational and societal changes to promote sustainability**
Instituting programs and policies	Establishment the Environmental Management Committee
Putting environmental interests first	Terminate or rescind the agreements with those who violate the specified regulations and cause significant impact on the environment
Lobbying and activism	Advocate legislative initiatives that allow at least the option for manufacturers to recover their own brand products

Note. Adapted from Ref. [5]. Copyright 2022 by Wang et al. [5] and Wiernik et al. [19]. Copyright 2012 by Wiernik et al. [19]

Table 1.
Organizational environmental sustainability initiatives taxonomy.

a commonly used metric closed link to softmax to evaluate accuracy for multi-class classification. The main advantage of the metric is to proportionally penalize incorrect predictions based on the probability that a prediction differs from the actual class. Lastly, the model also utilizes early stopping, where it monitors validation loss and stop the training process when the metric stops decreasing for a few epochs. The number of epochs the model monitors (i.e., patience) are set to 3 for RNN, 5 for BERT. Both models also restore the best weight, where the weight in the epoch that achieves lowest validation loss is kept.

2.1.4 Performance evaluation

The trained models were evaluated on the test set using three metrics: precision, recall, and F1 score. Precision measures the proportion of correctly predicted positive instances among all predicted positives, while recall quantifies the model's ability to identify all actual positive instances. The F1 score, calculated as the harmonic mean of precision and recall, provides a balanced measure of the model's overall performance. We selected the weighted average F-1 score as the main model performance metric to ensure that results are not overly influenced by categories with fewer examples. The complete script used for data preprocessing, model training and performance evaluation is available at https://osf.io/4gnsp/.

2.2 Results for experiment 1

The classification performance of two deep learning models, along with the results of three shallow ML models reported in Wang et al., is presented in **Table 2**. The BERT model achieved a weighted F1-score of 0.74 on the test set, outperforming the

Organizational environmental sustainability initiative categories	Traditional ML			Deep learning	
	Max entropy	SVC	MultiNB	RNN	BERT
Changing how work is done	0.43	0.47	0.29	0.32	0.60
Choosing responsible alternatives	0.66	0.65	0.58	0.59	0.71
Creating sustainable products and processes	0.66	0.67	0.61	0.57	0.67
Educating and training for sustainability	0.67	0.69	0.35	0.54	0.86
Embracing innovation for sustainability	0.22	0.20	0.00	0.00	0.00
Encouraging and supporting others	0.58	0.55	0.46	0.45	0.68
Instituting programs and policies	0.76	0.76	0.69	0.72	0.82
Lobbying and activism	0.19	0.24	0.00	0.00	0.00
Monitoring environmental impact	0.78	0.77	0.71	0.78	0.86
Preventing pollution	0.65	0.66	0.59	0.61	0.81
Putting environmental interests first	0.19	0.24	0.00	0.00	0.00
Recycling	0.74	0.75	0.58	0.68	0.72
Reducing use	0.59	0.56	0.48	0.54	0.77
Repurposing	0.57	0.50	0.00	0.00	0.37
Reusing	0.42	0.33	0.00	0.00	0.00
Strengthening ecosystems	0.66	0.71	0.57	0.55	0.82
Weighted average	0.67	0.67	0.56	0.59	0.74

Note. Max Entropy = Maximum Entropy, a type of logistic regression classifier; SVC = Support Vector Classifier, a model that separates data points using hyperplanes; MultiNB = Multinomial Naïve Bayes, a probabilistic classifier often used for text data; RNN = Recurrent Neural Network, a deep learning model designed for sequential data like text; BERT = Bidirectional Encoder Representations from Transformers, a deep learning model that captures context in text by reading in both directions.

Table 2.
Weighted F-1 scores of traditional machine learning (ML) and deep learning models.

best-performing shallow model, the Maximum Entropy classifier, which had a mean F1-score of 0.67. In contrast, the RNN model performed significantly worse, with a mean F1-score of 0.59. **Table A1** details precision, recall, and F1-scores for each initiative category. The BERT model performed best on the categories "Educating and Training for Sustainability" and "Monitoring Environmental Impact," both achieving F1-scores of 0.86, followed by "Instituting Programs and Policies" and "Strengthening Ecosystems" with F1-scores of 0.82. However, for some categories such as "Reusing", BERT model had much lower F1 scores compared to the Max entropy model (0.31 vs. 0.54). These results suggest that while BERT generally outperforms simpler models, it struggles with certain minor categories. This issue is particularly pronounced for categories with extremely low base rates, where both the BERT and RNN models faced significant challenges in classification: both models had an F1-score of 0 for the four and five initiative categories with the lowest base rates. Overall, these findings highlight BERT's advantage in general classification tasks but also reveal its limitations in handling underrepresented categories where data scarcity impacts model performance.

3. Experiment 2

The second experiment focused on using LLMs to classify the same set of initiatives. For comparison purposes, we used the same train-validation-test split set to ensure the results are comparable with the deep learning models. In this section, we will introduce the model used and describe our specific research design.

Our experiment used two popular base language models (GPT-3.5-turbo and GPT-4) combined with four common prompting techniques: zero-shot, zero-shot with Chain of Thought (CoT), few-shot, and few-shot with CoT. Zero-shot prompting involves presenting the model with an initiative and the initiative taxonomy without providing any examples, relying solely on its pre-trained knowledge to generate a response. That is, this model relies only on its pre-trained knowledge to classify the initiative. Zero-shot with Chain of Thought (CoT) prompting extends this approach by encouraging the model to explain its classification reasoning step by step, which has been shown to lead to more accurate and interpretable answers. Few-shot prompting, by contrast, provides the model with a handful of example initiatives and their human-coded categories to help it recognize patterns and improve its responses. Few-shot with CoT combines both these strategies by supplying the model examples and eliciting explicit reasoning steps.

Additionally, we explored fine-tuning the GPT-3.5-turbo model using the training and validation sets. This process involved preparing our dataset in the required JSONL files, where each entry included an initiative and its correct classification category. We then uploaded the dataset to OpenAI's fine-tuning platform, where the model was trained on our specific data to improve its domain-specific accuracy and performance. We did not fine-tune the GPT-4 model as fine-tuning provides minimal performance gains for GPT-4 due to its larger model size. Our design resulted in a total of 9 experiment conditions. The complete script used for GPT simulation and performance evaluation is available at https://osf.io/4gnsp/.

3.1 Results for experiment 2

The F-1 score summaries for all GPT models can be found in **Table 3**. Based on the zero-shot, no-CoT GPT-3.5-turbo model, adding examples (few-shot) or reasoning

	GPT 3.5				GPT 4				
	0-shot	**Few-shot**	**0-shot**	**Few-shot**	**0-shot**	**0-shot**	**Few-shot**	**0 shot**	**Few-shot**
	No CoT	No CoT	CoT	CoT	Fine-tuned	No CoT	No CoT	CoT	CoT
Changing how work is done	0.10	0.23	0.13	0.30	0.60	0.20	0.24	0.39	0.16
Choosing responsible alternatives	0.20	0.22	0.19	0.39	0.78	0.43	0.36	0.42	0.18
Creating sustainable products &processes	0.35	0.34	0.33	0.28	0.72	0.44	0.27	0.33	0.42
Educating and training for sustainability	0.37	0.59	0.48	0.55	0.81	0.59	0.56	0.50	0.52
Embracing innovation for sustainability	0.11	0.07	0.10	0.11	0.40	0.06	0.08	0.13	0.07
Encouraging and supporting others	0.29	0.42	0.32	0.34	0.67	0.41	0.39	0.38	0.27
Instituting programs and policies	0.31	0.32	0.21	0.18	0.84	0.54	0.54	0.49	0.45
Lobbying and activism	0.27	0.46	0.17	0.33	0.25	0.18	0.17	0.29	0.00
Monitoring environmental impact	0.43	0.45	0.52	0.43	0.87	0.65	0.68	0.62	0.61
Preventing pollution	0.50	0.53	0.44	0.36	0.75	0.52	0.54	0.51	0.54
Putting environmental interests first	0.01	0.01	0.01	0.00	0.77	0.00	0.00	0.00	0.00
Recycling	0.42	0.60	0.44	0.38	0.76	0.70	0.70	0.71	0.68
Reducing use	0.22	0.36	0.32	0.37	0.78	0.47	0.42	0.50	0.44
Repurposing	0.18	0.38	0.27	0.36	0.42	0.15	0.39	0.29	0.20
Reusing	0.22	0.15	0.25	0.21	0.52	0.36	0.31	0.29	0.25
Strengthening ecosystems	0.26	0.43	0.31	0.48	0.80	0.61	0.64	0.68	0.66
Weighted average	**0.32**	**0.38**	**0.33**	**0.34**	**0.77**	**0.50**	**0.48**	**0.48**	**0.43**

Table 3.
Classification Performance Comparison Across 9 Model Configurations: Weighted F1 Scores.

steps (CoT) modestly improves performance. Among the four prompting strategies, few-shot prompting without CoT provides the largest gain for GPT-3.5-turbo, increasing the weighted F1-score by 6 percentage points (from 0.32 to 0.38). However, for GPT-4, this pattern reverses: the simplest approach—zero-shot prompting without CoT—achieves the highest F1-score (0.50), while more complex prompting methods yield lower scores, with few-shot CoT performing 7 percentage points worse. Overall, GPT-4 consistently outperforms GPT-3.5-turbo across prompting strategies, with zero-shot prompting producing the largest improvement (a jump from 0.32 to 0.50). Nonetheless, all non-fine-tuned GPT models, regardless of prompting strategy, fall short of the performance achieved by the fine-tuned GPT-3.5 model and also underperform relative to the best shallow machine learning model (e.g., Naïve Bayes).

In contrast, the fine-tuned GPT-3.5-turbo model achieved the highest overall performance, with a weighted F1-score of 0.77, outperforming all other models. Notably, fine-tuning led to a substantial improvement over its base versions, increasing the F1-score by at least 0.30 in every category. Furthermore, all categories in the fine-tuned GPT-3.5-turbo model recorded F1-scores of 0.40 or higher, except for "Lobbying and Activism" (F1-score 0.25), which had the lowest base rate. These findings indicate that even the most advanced models show limitations when classifying initiatives with very low base rates. The results also suggest that fine-tuning significantly enhances performance, especially in commonly represented categories.

It is also worth noting that model hallucination, where the model generates nonexistent or invalid categories, was observed in all GPT-4 prompting configurations except the two without CoT prompting. Additionally, failure to classify certain initiatives occurred in all but one model (zero-shot GPT-4). In contrast, neither the deep learning models (RNN, BERT) nor the shallow models exhibited these issues, as their architectures are specifically designed for structured classification tasks.

4. Discussion

Our research yielded several key insights into the application of computer science algorithms for content analysis. First, advanced models, particularly those leveraging attention and transformer architectures, demonstrated superior accuracy in categorizing environmental initiatives compared to traditional machine learning models. This result aligns with the well-documented success of transformers across various fields. Second, our findings highlight the substantial performance gains of fine-tuned GPT models over their base versions with different prompting techniques. This underscores the effectiveness of domain-specific databases over prompting alone for specialized tasks, reaffirming the continued need for fine-tuning in large language models. Finally, our study demonstrated deep learning's ability to overcome two major challenges associated with shallow models: the need for intensive feature engineering and comparatively lower performance.

Among the lower-performing models, we were surprised to find that the RNN model underperformed compared to the SVM and Max Entropy models. This result may be attributed to the small dataset used for training. Previous research showed that deep learning models surpass traditional machine learning models as sample size increases, exhibiting continuous improvement, whereas traditional methods reach a performance ceiling (see **Figure 1** for a visual illustration) [20]. Moreover, the performance of base GPT models can be understood in the context of task complexity.

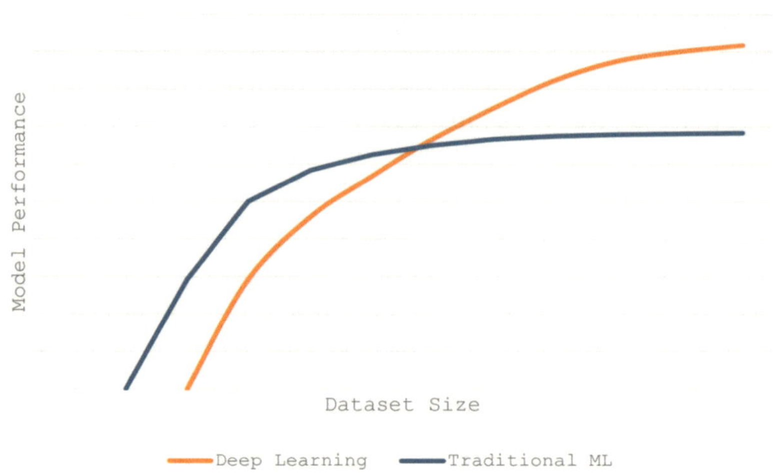

Figure 1.
Model performance of deep learning vs. other machine learning algorithms as a function of sample size. Adapted from Ref. [20].

Advanced vocabulary and linguistic proficiency do not necessarily translate to domain-specific understanding. However, pre-trained models like BERT and GPT deviate from this trend, as they already possess a strong grasp of natural language. In these cases, additional input serves as domain-specific knowledge, making the training set significantly more efficient for fine-tuning.

When comparing fine-tuned GPT-3.5-turbo with the BERT model, GPT achieves better overall performance; however, BERT offers comparable results with significantly greater efficiency and flexibility. First, BERT can be deployed on personal computers or freely accessible platforms such as Google Colab, Kaggle Kernels, and Jupyter Cloud Notebook, which many researchers already have access to. In contrast, GPT relies on an API-based service that charges users per token, making large-scale tasks expensive. For instance, fine-tuning GPT-3.5-turbo on our dataset (9656 examples) with three epochs cost $20, and costs scale rapidly with larger sample sizes. Second, deep learning remains more flexible than GPT models, as researchers can modify model architectures for different tasks—an advantage that traditional deep learning retains over large language models (LLMs).

The rise of Generative Pre-trained Transformer (GPT) models has sparked debate over the relevance of traditional deep learning approaches. In this chapter, we argue that deep learning remains relevant for several reasons. First, deep learning continues to outperform many GPT models. As demonstrated in our research, models like BERT can achieve performance comparable to the best fine-tuned GPT model. Second, deep learning offers greater customizability, allowing researchers to tailor model architectures and parameters to specific tasks and constraints. This adaptability is particularly beneficial for specialized tasks like content analysis. Third, while personal computers lack the resources to train LLMs from scratch, expertise in deep learning remains valuable for customizing and fine-tuning smaller, personalized LLMs in the future. Finally, deep learning is significantly more data efficient. LLMs require terabytes of data for training, whereas deep learning models operate on gigabytes and can run on personal computers. For focused, domain-specific tasks, deep learning models are not only cheaper and faster to train but also offer the flexibility to scale based on research needs by adjusting dataset size.

4.1 Key contributions and limitations

Our findings provide significant insights to behavioral science and psychological research methods. First, we conducted a direct comparison of traditional machine learning, deep learning, and large language models using an identical organizational psychology dataset, providing researchers with practical guidance for model selection and deployment. Second, we demonstrate that, with pre-trained models, a moderately sized psychological dataset can achieve human-level classification accuracy without manual feature engineering. Finally, while overfitting is a common concern in deep learning applications, we present a straightforward introduction to these methods, aimed at increasing researchers' confidence in applying and refining such models.

While this study makes valuable contributions, it has several limitations. First, there is still progress to be made in helping our researchers build model architectures and address complex issues such as overfitting. A hands-on tutorial would provide an effective approach to introduce these advanced machine learning topics. Although in these models, the need for extensive feature engineering is reduced, achieving human-level performance still requires domain expertise in computer science, particularly for fine-tuning models.

Second, we did not determine the minimum sample size needed for deep learning models to achieve high accuracy. Addressing this would require access to a larger dataset than the one used in this study. For the domain of organizational environmental sustainability, even where data on environmental sustainability initiatives exist, table schemas and category frameworks often differ. This challenge is common to content analysis tasks, especially when categories and coding standards are still under debate.

Finally, the scope of our GPT experiments was constrained by time and budget. While we explored nine model configurations, many additional combinations remain unexplored. For instance, future work could examine the performance of a fine-tuned GPT-4 model or identify the minimum dataset size required to achieve human-level accuracy for both BERT and fine-tuned GPT models.

In summary, while this study lays important groundwork for applying deep learning and GPT models to the classification of environmental initiatives, addressing these limitations will require expanded fine-tuning efforts, larger and more diverse datasets, and further research. These steps are critical for fully harnessing AI's potential to advance environmental research and action.

4.2 Proposed future directions

The exploration of deep learning models for categorizing environmental initiatives reveals opportunities to further enhance model performance and reliability through advanced methodologies. A promising next step is the implementation of ensemble models, where multiple models collaborate to improve decision-making. Drawing from research on human judgment, ensemble models apply the "wisdom of crowds" principle, where diverse decision-makers collectively achieve more accurate and robust outcomes than any single expert. This approach is particularly valuable in complex domains such as environmental initiative categorization, where individual models may struggle to fully capture intricate data relationships.

Another critical area for future research is the advancement of GPT models. While future versions of GPT are likely to deliver improved performance, they will also impose greater computational demands and environmental costs. The energy consumption associated with large language models (LLMs) is already a growing concern and is expected to become even more pressing. Researchers will need to weigh the benefits of LLMs against the imperative for responsible and sustainable AI practices.

Furthermore, interdisciplinary collaboration presents a promising solution to the challenge of sparse datasets. Given that content analysis spans multiple fields, integrating deep learning expertise from diverse disciplines could lead to more innovative approaches. Partnerships between machine learning specialists and researchers in the social and behavioral sciences can help address complex problems more effectively, ensuring that GPT models are developed and applied ethically, responsibly, and in alignment with human values.

Finally, as computational approaches to computer-aided content analysis (CACA) incorporating machine learning continue to evolve, existing guidelines for CACA should be revisited and updated. Further research is also needed to evaluate the validity and reliability of deep learning methods in this domain.

5. Conclusions

This study demonstrated the potential of deep learning and large language models to automate and improve the classification of organizational environmental initiatives. While fine-tuned GPT models and BERT outperformed traditional approaches, each method revealed distinct trade-offs in terms of performance, interpretability, and resource requirements. Our findings highlight the need for continued exploration of hybrid models, fine-tuning strategies, and interdisciplinary collaboration to fully leverage AI in content analysis. Future work should also address ethical, environmental, and methodological challenges to ensure the responsible application of these technologies in organizational research.

Conflict of interest

The authors declare no conflict of interest.

Appendix

	RNN-LSTM		
Category	**Precision**	**Recall**	**F1-Score**
Changing how work is done	0.41	0.26	0.32
Choosing responsible alternatives	0.58	0.59	0.59
Creating sustainable products and processes	0.51	0.65	0.57
Educating and training for sustainability	0.61	0.49	0.54
Embracing innovation for sustainability	0.00	0.00	0.00

	RNN-LSTM		
Category	**Precision**	**Recall**	**F1-Score**
Encouraging and supporting others	0.45	0.46	0.45
Instituting programs and policies	0.64	0.81	0.72
Lobbying and activism	0.00	0.00	0.00
Monitoring environmental impact	0.76	0.80	0.78
Preventing pollution	0.59	0.62	0.61
Putting environmental interests first	0.00	0.00	0.00
Recycling	0.65	0.71	0.68
Reducing use	0.63	0.47	0.54
Repurposing	0.00	0.00	0.00
Reusing	0.00	0.00	0.00
Strengthening ecosystems	0.75	0.44	0.55
Micro-average	0.61	0.61	0.61
Weighted average	**0.59**	**0.61**	**0.59**
BERT			
Changing how work is done	0.65	0.55	0.60
Choosing responsible alternatives	0.68	0.75	0.71
Creating sustainable products and processes	0.70	0.65	0.67
Educating and training for sustainability	0.83	0.90	0.86
Embracing innovation for sustainability	0.00	0.00	0.00
Encouraging and supporting others	0.68	0.67	0.68
Instituting programs and policies	0.79	0.84	0.82
Lobbying and activism	0.00	0.00	0.00
Monitoring environmental impact	0.79	0.93	0.86
Preventing pollution	0.80	0.81	0.81
Putting environmental interests first	0.00	0.00	0.00
Recycling	0.73	0.71	0.72
Reducing use	0.83	0.72	0.77
Repurposing	0.60	0.27	0.37
Reusing	0.00	0.00	0.00
Strengthening ecosystems	0.81	0.83	0.82
Micro-average	0.75	0.75	0.75
Weighted average	**0.74**	**0.75**	**0.74**

Table A1.
Precision, recall and F1-scores for RNN-LSTM and BERT models.

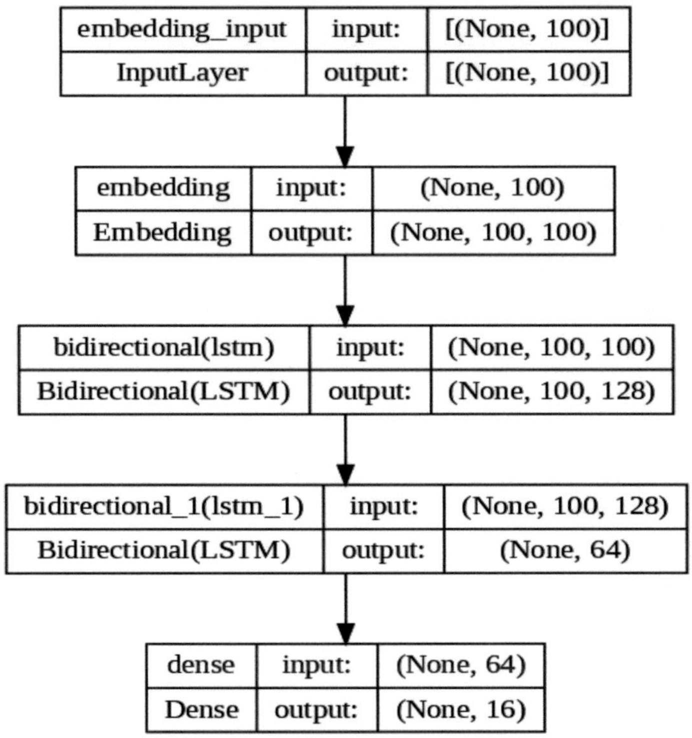

Figure A1.
Architecture of RNN-LSTM model.

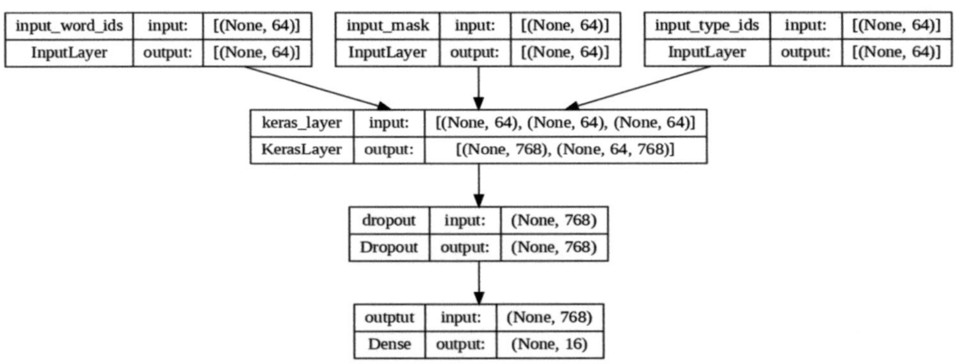

Figure A2.
Architecture of BERT model.

Deep Learning Applications for Analysis of Unstructured Data
DOI: http://dx.doi.org/10.5772/intechopen.1010729

Author details

Zekai Wei[1], Yilei Wang[2*] and Deniz S. Ones[3]

1 Amazon LLC, Seattle, WA, United States

2 Shanghai Institute of AI for Education, East China Normal University, China

3 Department of Psychology, University of Minnesota – Twin Cities, United States

*Address all correspondence to: wangyilei@mail.ecnu.edu.cn

References

[1] Krippendorff K. Validity in content analysis. Computerstrategien Für Die Kommunikationsanalyse. 1980;**291**:69-112. Available from: https://repository.upenn.edu/handle/20.500.14332/1940

[2] Popping R. Computer-Assisted Text Analysis. London: SAGE; 2000

[3] Pollach I. Taming textual data: The contribution of corpus linguistics to computer-aided text analysis. Organizational Research Methods. 2012;**15**:263-287. DOI: 10.1177/1094428111417451

[4] Hickman L, Thapa S, Tay L, Cao M, Srinivasan P. Text preprocessing for text mining in organizational research: Review and recommendations. Organizational Research Methods. 2022;**25**(1):114-146. DOI: 10.1177/1094428120971683

[5] Wang Y, Tian J, Yazar Y, Ones D, Landers R. Using natural language processing and machine learning to replace human content coders. Psychological Methods. 2022;**29**(6):1148-1163. DOI: 10.1037/met0000518

[6] Alissa M, Sim K, Hart E. Algorithm selection using deep learning without feature extraction. Proceedings of the Genetic and Evolutionary Computation Conference. 2019:198-206. DOI: 10.1145/3321707.3321845

[7] Allen-Zhu Z, Li Y. Backward feature correction: How deep learning performs deep (hierarchical) learning. Proceedings of Thirty Sixth Conference on Learning Theory. 2023:4598-4598. Available from: https://proceedings.mlr.press/v195/allen-zhu23a.html

[8] Xie X, Niu J, Liu X, Chen Z, Tang S, Yu S. A survey on incorporating domain knowledge into deep learning for medical image analysis. Medical Image Analysis. 2021;**69**:101985. DOI: 10.1016/j.media.2021.101985

[9] Trafimow D, Uhalt J. The alleged tradeoff between explanatory breadth and predictive power. Theory & Psychology. 2015;**25**:833-840. DOI: 10.1177/0959354315591052

[10] Yarkoni T, Westfall J. Choosing prediction over explanation in psychology: Lessons from machine learning. Perspectives on Psychological Science. 2017;**12**(6):1100-1122. DOI: 10.1177/1745691617693393

[11] Ones DS, Dilchert S, Wiernik BM, Klein RM. Environmental sustainability at work. In: Ones DS, Anderson N, Viswesvaran C, Sinangil HK, editors. The SAGE Handbook of Industrial, Work and Organizational Psychology. 2nd ed. Vol. 3. London, United Kingdom: Sage; 2018. pp. 351-373. DOI: 10.4135/9781473914964.n17

[12] Ones D, Dilchert S. Environmental sustainability at work: A call to action. Industrial and Organizational Psychology. 2012;**5**:444-466. DOI: 10.1111/j.1754-9434.2012.01478.x

[13] Tian J, Ones DS. Comparing environmental initiatives of French and German companies. In: Cross-Cultural Investigations of Organizational pro-Environmental Initiatives. Society for Industrial and Organizational Psychology Annual Conference, Washington, D.C. 2019

[14] Wang Y, Ones DS. Environmental sustainability in Chinese companies: Are high-polluters addressing their impacts? In: Dilchert S, editor. Cross-Cultural

Investigations of Organizational pro-Environmental Initiatives. Symposium Conducted at the Annual Meeting of the Society for Industrial and Organizational Psychology, Chicago, IL. 2018

[15] Yazar Y, Ones DS. Investigating the green initiatives of the MENA region companies. In: Dilchert S, editor. Cross-Cultural Investigations of Organizational pro-Environmental Initiatives. Symposium Conducted at the Annual Meeting of the Society for Industrial and Organizational Psychology, Chicago, IL. 2018

[16] D'Mello S, Klein R, Ones DS, Dilchert S, Wiernik BM, Hill L. Organizations go green: A behaviorally informed taxonomy of organizational sustainability. In: Dilchert S, editor. Organizational and Group Differences in Environmentally Responsible Employee Behaviors. Symposium Conducted at the Annual Meeting of the Society for Industrial and Organizational Psychology, Atlanta, GA. 2010. DOI: 10.1037/e518392013-387

[17] Ones D, Dilchert S. Employee green behaviors. In: Managing HR for Environmental Sustainability. San Francisco: Jossey-Bass/Wiley; 2012. pp. 85-116

[18] Ones DS, Dilchert S. Green behaviors of workers: A taxonomy for the green economy. In: Dilchert S, Ones DS, editors. Environmentally Friendly Worker Behaviors, Senior Leader Wrongdoing, and National Level Outcomes. Symposium Conducted at the Annual Meeting of the Academy of Management, Chicago, Illinois. 2009

[19] Wiernik BM, Ones DS, D'Mello S, Dilchert S, Klein R. A taxonomy of organizational environmental initiatives: Psychological foundations Poster presented at the Society of Personality and Social Psychology Sustainability Psychology Preconference, San Diego, CA; 2012

[20] Ng W, Minasny B, de Sousa Mendes W, Demattê J. The influence of training sample size on the accuracy of deep learning models for the prediction of soil properties with near-infrared spectroscopy data. The Soil. 2020;**6**:565-578. DOI: 10.5194/soil-6-565-2020

Section 2

New Psychometric Tests Studies

Chapter 5

Reviewing the Translated and Validated Scales in Positive Psychology in Sports within Arabic-Speaking Countries

Marei Ahmed

Abstract

Positive psychology in the sports field is an emerging discipline that offers valuable insights for practitioners, coaches, and professionals working with diverse populations, including young athletes, adults, the elderly, and individuals with special needs. This chapter reviews existing research on the translation, adaptation, and validation of positive psychology scales in sports across different cultural contexts, with a specific focus on the scarcity of studies within Arabic cultures. Findings indicate that well-established methodologies are commonly used for scale validation, employing various statistical techniques to assess psychometric properties. These approaches reflect the diversity of theoretical models in the field. However, the review also highlights the limited application of Item Response Theory (IRT), with only a few studies utilizing one, two, or three IRT models. This gap underscores the need for further research incorporating advanced psychometric methods to enhance the validity and reliability of positive psychology assessments in sports.

Keywords: validation scales, psychometric properties, positive psychology, sports field, Arabic speaking

1. Introduction

The interdisciplinary field offers a unique framework for enhancing athletes' performance, well-being, and overall development by focusing on their strengths, virtues, and optimal functioning. In recent years, researchers have adapted and validated various positive psychology scales in diverse cultural contexts, including Arabic-speaking populations [1]. These scales assess a range of constructs, such as character strengths, gratitude, and mindfulness, and can provide valuable insights into athletes' psychological profiles [2–5]. However, a significant gap in the literature lies in the limited use of IRT models to analyze these scales. IRT offers a powerful statistical framework for evaluating the psychometric properties of assessments and can provide more precise and nuanced information about individual differences in athlete characteristics [6].

1.1 Positive psychology

Positive psychology has shifted the focus of psychologists by creating a practical framework that explores "what actions lead to well-being, positive individuals, and thriving communities" [7]. It is a scientific study of human flourishing, focusing on the positive aspects and strengths of individuals and communities as pathways to well-being. Martin Seligman, a leading proponent of the theory, has played a significant role in steering psychology away from an exclusive focus on pathology and illness. His work emphasizes the importance of supporting clients in identifying their strengths and setting goals to guide meaningful behavior [8].

The goal of positive psychology is to provide individuals and society with tools to flourish rather than dwell on mental ill-health, which has traditionally been the primary focus of psychology. Seligman [8] believed that a research-based approach could guide individuals toward flourishing and a satisfying life while also raising the standard for the human condition. Over the past decade, numerous branches of positive psychology have emerged and evolved, according to the official website of the International Positive Psychology Association. These branches include: (1) positive health and wellness, (2) positive clinical psychology (recently renamed positive clinical psychology), (3) positive education, (4) work and organizations, (5) a branch for students across various sub-specialties, (6) positive neuroscience (currently discontinued), and (7) spirituality and meaning, which emphasizes spiritual and religious connections without regard to racial, ethnic, gender, or cultural backgrounds ("IPPA", [9]).

1.2 Exercise and sport psychology

Exercise psychology and sports psychology explore the scientific influence of psychological factors on participation and performance in sports, exercise, and physical activity. Sports psychologists primarily focus on two key areas: (a) assisting athletes in utilizing psychological principles to enhance their mental well-being and performance and (b) investigating the impact of involvement in sports and physical activity on psychological development, health, and overall well-being throughout their lifespan. These disciplines have evolved, expanding from a primary focus on performance enhancement to encompass the promotion of health and well-being through regular physical activity. This evolution has led to the emergence of exercise psychology as a distinct field, often merging it with health psychology [10].

1.3 Positive psychology in sports

Positive psychology can be effectively applied to various aspects of sports and physical activity. However, it is crucial to acknowledge the diverse contexts, activities, and meanings associated with sports and physical activity. Given the broad spectrum of activities encompassed by the term "sport," providing a single, definitive definition is challenging. A broader perspective defines sport as encompassing all forms of physical activity, whether casual or organized, that aim to improve physical fitness, enhance mental well-being, foster social relationships, and achieve competitive success at various levels.

Positive psychology in sports aims to enhance performance through competition while simultaneously improving well-being and happiness, which are often underrepresented in Arab societies. Furthermore, the research tools employed in positive psychology can be adapted for use in educational sports settings to measure various variables and contribute to personal fulfillment and higher quality of life [11, 12].

No doubt, positive psychology in sports is a specialized and emerging field that offers multifaceted contributions to recreational, educational, and competitive sports. Its primary objective is to elucidate the complex, interactive relationships between positive psychology and the various facets of sports. This branch aims not only to enhance the performance and development of athletes but also to support individuals, teams, and staff in achieving their optimal level of well-being, ultimately leading to a better, more prosperous life throughout their lifespan. This field provides valuable knowledge and international research for professionals and researchers, including psychologists, in areas related to physical activity at all levels. This knowledge can be applied to individuals of all ages, including children, adults, and the elderly, as well as those with special needs, by understanding and utilizing theoretical models, research findings, and practical suggestions [1, 12, 13].

2. Methodology

To ensure a comprehensive and structured approach to the review, a clear methodology was employed. Below are the key methodological steps taken:

2.1 Type and nature of reviewed studies

This study adopts a narrative review approach, meaning that it synthesizes existing literature without adhering to the strict methodological framework of systematic reviews. The goal is to identify key themes, trends, and research gaps related to positive psychology in sports within Arabic-speaking countries.

It is important to clarify that while the methodological approach of this study is a narrative review, the majority of the reviewed studies are instrumental studies primarily focused on scale validation and psychometric assessment. As such, this review provides a structured synthesis of psychometric research, analyzing the methods, findings, and implications of these validation studies within the field of positive psychology in sports.

2.2 Search strategy

The literature search was conducted using EBSCOhost and Google Scholar, two widely recognized academic databases. The following keywords were used to identify relevant studies: "positive psychology in sports", "validation scale in positive psychology", "validation scale in sports", "positive psychology scale Arabic athletes", and "Adaptation scales in positive psychology sports". Filters have been applied to include peer-reviewed journal articles, conference proceedings, and dissertations published between 2010 and 2024.

2.3 Inclusion and exclusion criteria

2.3.1 Inclusion criteria

Studies published in English, Arabic, or French were selected. Articles focusing on the translation, adaptation, or validation of positive psychology scales in sports were specifically targeted. Additionally, research involving Arabic-speaking athlete populations was included. Only empirical studies providing psychometric evaluations were considered for inclusion.

2.3.2 Exclusion criteria

Conversely, non-peer-reviewed articles, such as blog posts and editorials, were excluded. Studies that did not specifically focus on both positive psychology and sports were omitted. Research lacking clear psychometric analysis, such as validity and reliability, was similarly excluded.

2.4 Selection and analysis process

Following the predefined search strategy, a three-step selection process was conducted. Firstly, initial filtering was performed based on the relevance of the title and abstract to the study objectives. Articles that passed this stage then underwent a full-text review to ensure methodological rigor. Lastly, key information, including the study design, assessed psychometric properties, and major findings, was extracted for thematic analysis.

The selected studies were chosen to provide a diverse and representative overview of positive psychology research in sports within Arabic-speaking contexts. Particular emphasis was placed on articles that followed rigorous psychometric validation methods, ensuring their applicability to Arabic-speaking athletes.

3. Results

3.1 Studies on non-Arabic samples

Several studies have focused on validating various psychological scales in sports contexts, emphasizing their reliability and validity across diverse populations. The following table summarizes studies found on positive psychology scales in sports.

The studies summarized in **Table 1** generally report acceptable levels of reliability for the instruments evaluated. For example, Santi et al. [14] found acceptable reliability for the Athlete Psychological Well-Being Inventory (APWBI), and Nogueira López et al. [15] confirmed that the adapted Short Grit Scale (Grit-S) demonstrated acceptable reliability among amateur runners. In a revision of the Gratitude Questionnaire-Six-Item Form (GQ-6), Fung [16] revised it to a five-item version (GQ-5) for improved reliability. Additionally, both Borrajo et al. [17] and Pereira da Silva et al. [18] reported that their adapted scales showed reliability within their respective samples.

The scales evaluated across the studies exhibit strong validity evidence. Sood and Puri [19] validated the Spanish version of the Psychological Capital Questionnaire (PCQ) and confirmed a four-factor structure. Borrajo et al. [17] also adapted and validated the PCQ for athletes, supporting its validity in a sports context. Studies like those by Peixoto et al. [20] and Lichtenstein et al. [21] provided validation for the Passion Scale, confirming a two-factor structure in Brazil and a three-dimensional structure in Denmark, respectively. Similarly, Nascimento-Junior et al. [22] and Bicalho et al. [23] presented evidence supporting the validity of the Life Skills Scale for Sport (LSSS) and the 5Cs model of youth development across cultures.

Author(s)	Year	Instrument evaluated	Sample	Key findings
Sood and Puri	2023	Psychological Capital Questionnaire (PCQ)	Spanish-speaking athletes	Validated Spanish version; confirmed four-factor structure.
Borrajo et al.	2022	Psychological Capital Questionnaire (PCQ)	Athletes	Adapted and validated for sports; demonstrated reliability and validity.
Santi et al.	2024	Athlete Psychological Well-Being Inventory (APWBI)	English-speaking athletes	Acceptable reliability and construct validity.
Nogueira López et al.	2023	Short Grit Scale (Grit-S)	Amateur runners	Adapted for runners; demonstrated acceptable validity and reliability.
Pereira da Silva et al.	2022	Self-Compassion Scale (SCS)	Young Brazilian athletes	Validated across genders; supports healthy relationships in sports.
Peixoto et al.	2019	Passion Scale	Brazilian athletes	Confirmed two-factor structure; measurement invariance across competitive levels.
Lichtenstein et al.	2020	Passion Scale	Danish fitness sample	Revealed a three-dimensional structure.
Salama-Younes and Hashim	2018	Passion Scale	French athletes	Validated through CFA; showed subjective vitality mediates passion and life satisfaction.
Fung	2024	Gratitude Questionnaire-Six-Item Form (GQ-6)	Chinese sample	Revised to a five-item version (GQ-5) for improved reliability.
Nascimento-Junior et al.	2020	Life Skills Scale for Sport (LSSS)	Athletes	Validated in diverse cultures; supports resilience and growth.
Bicalho et al.	2022	5Cs model of youth development	Athletes	Confirmed validity and psychometric properties in different cultural contexts.

Table 1.
Summary of reviewed studies on positive psychology scales in sports.

3.2 Statistical and research methods used for translation, adaptation, and validation of positive psychology scales in sports

Positive psychology in sports research employs a diverse array of statistical methodologies to develop and validate measurement instruments. One commonly utilized approach is Exploratory and Confirmatory Factor Analysis. These techniques are employed to examine the underlying factor structure of scales and assess their fit with theoretical models.

Another key methodology is Structural Equation Modeling (SEM), which allows for the investigation of complex relationships between multiple variables, such as the interplay between positive emotions, motivation, and performance. Additionally, Measurement Invariance Testing is utilized to ensure that the scale consistently measures the same construct across different groups, such as male versus female athletes or individuals from different cultural backgrounds.

Reliability is also a crucial aspect of these methodologies, specifically focusing on internal consistency and test-retest stability. Internal consistency refers to the consistency of the results across items within a test, while test-retest stability ensures that a test produces stable and repeatable results under the same conditions.

These methods have been applied in studies examining a range of positive psychological constructs in athletes and physical education students, including optimism, explanatory style, subjective well-being, enjoyment, resilience, passion types, and positive and negative effects.

3.3 Studies on the development and validation of positive psychology scales in Arabic countries

In Arabic countries, EBSCO and Google Scholar were used for the review, and it was found that very few studies followed a rigorous method to translate and validate the scales. This section highlights several key studies that have focused on developing and validating positive psychology scales specifically for Arabic-speaking athletes. The following key findings in **Table 2** can only be found in EBSCO and Google Scholar.

The studies present strong evidence of reliability across the evaluated instruments. For example, Salama-Younes [6, 24–26] reported good internal reliability for the Psychological Flourishing Scale (PFS) among Egyptian student-athletes [27], while

Author(s)	Year	Instrument evaluated	Sample	Key findings
Salama-Younes	2011	Mental Health Continuum-Short Form (MHC-SF)	Egyptian adolescent athletes	Supported a three-factor model (emotional, psychological, social well-being); positive correlation with subjective vitality.
Salama-Younes	2014a, 2014b	Psychological Flourishing Scale (PFS)	Egyptian student-athletes	Demonstrated good structural validity and internal reliability; supported temporal stability and convergent validity.
Salama-Younes	2015	Passion Scale	790 older French adults (55–72)	Confirmed scale structure; subjective vitality mediates harmonious passion and life satisfaction.
Salama-Younes	2017	Arabic Psychological Flourishing Scale (PFS)	Egyptian sports college students	Strong internal reliability, moderate temporal stability, and convergent validity with well-established measures.
Mnadla et al.	2017	Positive and Negative Affect Schedule (PANAS-D)	519 Tunisian athletes	Supported two-factor structure (positive and negative affect); validated Arabic-Tunisian version.
Salama-Younes and Hashim	2018	Arabic Passion Scale	551 older Egyptian adults	Showed gender and activity group invariance; subjective vitality mediates harmonious passion and life satisfaction.
Abbassi et al.	2021	Physical Education Flow Questionnaire (PHFLOW)	Arabic-speaking students	Confirmed four-dimensional structure, strong internal consistency, and concurrent validity.

Author(s)	Year	Instrument evaluated	Sample	Key findings
Ali and Salama-Younes	2021	Flourishing Scale (FS)	Egyptian male Judo players	Strong structural validity; subjective vitality mediates the relationship between flourishing and life satisfaction.
Ben Salha et al.	2022	Mindfulness Inventory for Sport (MIS-TAM)	North African athletes	Confirmed three-factor structure (Awareness, Non-Judgment, Refocusing); good internal consistency.
Ahmed et al.	2024	Passion, Resilience, Life Satisfaction Scales	Older Moroccan distance runners	Path analysis confirmed that resilience mediates the relationship between passion and life satisfaction

Table 2.
Summary of reviewed studies on positive psychology scales in sports.

Mnandla et al. [28] confirmed the internal consistency of the Positive and Negative Affect Schedule (PANAS-D) in a Tunisian athlete sample. Similarly, Ben Salha et al. [29] established good internal consistency for the Mindfulness Inventory for Sport (MIS-TAM). These findings indicate that the instruments used are stable and reliable across various populations.

The validity of the instruments is well-supported by multiple studies. Salama-Younes [2, 3] found a positive correlation between the Mental Health Continuum-Short Form (MHC-SF) and subjective vitality, affirming its construct validity. The Psychological Flourishing Scale (PFS), evaluated in multiple studies by Salama-Younes [6, 24] and Ali and Salama-Younes [13], demonstrated good structural and convergent validity. The Arabic Passion Scale showed invariance across gender and activity groups [12], enhancing its validity in diverse contexts. Notably, Ahmed et al. [30] confirmed through path analysis that resilience mediates the relationship between passion and life satisfaction, further supporting the tools' construct validity in measuring complex psychological constructs.

4. Discussion

The review of the studies conducted on non-Arabic samples illustrates the adaptability and relevance of psychological instruments in diverse athlete populations, highlighting their validation across various cultural contexts and sports. The studies underscore the importance of tailoring psychological tools to fit specific groups, such as Spanish-speaking athletes or amateur runners, which can enhance their applicability and effectiveness (as seen in the works of Sood and Puri, [19], and Nogueira López et al. [15]). Moreover, confirming the psychometric properties of these scales not only facilitates a deeper understanding of athlete psychology but also encourages further research into resilience, well-being, and personal development in sports. Overall, the established reliability and validity of these instruments suggest they can be effectively utilized in both research and practical settings to support athlete mental health and performance.

Additionally, the review of studies on the development and validation of positive psychology scales in Arabic countries highlights the importance of culturally adapted psychological instruments in understanding mental health and well-being in athletic populations in North Africa and the Arab world. The consistent findings regarding the reliability and validity of these instruments underscore their potential use in both research and practical settings. Salama-Younes' work, in particular, showcases the integration of subjective vitality as a key mediating factor in the relationships between various psychological constructs, such as flourishing and life satisfaction. The confirmation of structural models across diverse samples reinforces the relevance of these scales in capturing the nuanced experiences of athletes. Overall, the studies provide valuable insights into the psychological dynamics of athletic populations and suggest that promoting practices such as mindfulness and passion can contribute to enhanced well-being and performance.

Furthermore, the studies collectively demonstrate ongoing efforts to establish the reliability and validity of various psychological scales in Arabic-speaking contexts, with a focus on athlete populations. These findings contribute to a growing body of research highlighting the importance of psychological well-being in sports and the need for culturally sensitive and linguistically appropriate assessment tools. These studies represent valuable contributions to the field, as they not only validate these tools for use in Arabic-speaking contexts but also enhance our understanding of psychological well-being in sports settings within these cultures. These findings highlight the crucial role of positive constructs such as resilience, passion, and mindfulness in athlete development. Ongoing research underscores the growing recognition of the importance of mental health and well-being in sports, particularly within non-Western cultures, and supports the potential for further integration of positive psychology principles into athletic training and development programs in Arabic-speaking regions.

5. Recommendations

Several internationally recognized frameworks ensure robust and credible processes, often recommended by organizations such as the World Health Organization (WHO) and the International Test Commission (ITC). In sport psychology, Vallerand and Halliwell [31] proposed a rigorous methodology for this purpose, and more recently, Cruchinho et al. [32] provided a practical guide aimed at the same objective. However, there is currently no single, universally mandated methodology for the translation and validation of psychological scales officially accredited by any global body. In Arabic-speaking countries, few studies have adhered to this rigorous methodology for translating and validating positive psychology scales in sports.

Drawing from these references, this chapter proposes an approach for this process, which can generally be illustrated in this section.

5.1 Recommended methodology for translating, adapting, and validating positive psychology scales for Arabic athletes

The general process of the proposed methodology begins with forward and backward translation to ensure linguistic and conceptual equivalence. This is followed by cultural adaptation, where items will be modified to align with the target population's cultural and social norms. Next, pretesting will be conducted to evaluate item clarity and relevance. This phase will involve psychological experts and linguists to ensure the items are appropriate and effective. Subsequently, the psychometric properties will be assessed. This will include evaluations of reliability, validity, and structural equivalence, ensuring that the measurement instruments are sound and reliable. Finally, the process will be thoroughly documented. This step will maintain transparency and ensure the process can be replicated in future studies.

The detailed methodology for Arabic contexts will be illustrated as follows.

5.2 Pre-translation phase

The pre-translation phase will begin with a comprehensive literature review. This will involve a thorough examination of existing literature on the identified scales to understand their psychometric characteristics and previous validation efforts within various cultural contexts. Additionally, any preexisting Arabic adaptations of these scales will be evaluated, with a focus on identifying their shortcomings. Following this, the selection of the most suitable scales will be undertaken. Relevant positive psychology scales to be translated will be identified, including the Flourishing Scale, Satisfaction with Life Scale, PANAS, Mindfulness Inventory for Sport, Passion Scale, and Attributional Style Questionnaire. It will be essential to ensure that the selected scales are suitable for sports contexts, considering the psychological constructs they measure, such as flourishing, life satisfaction, and mindfulness.

Cultural considerations will also be paramount. Experts in positive psychology, sports psychology, bilingualism, and cultural psychology will be engaged to ensure the cultural appropriateness of the scales for Arabic-speaking athletes. Potential cultural differences in how the constructs measured by the scales manifest in the Arabic athletic context will be identified and addressed accordingly.

5.3 Translation process

The translation process will begin with assembling a team of bilingual experts in Arabic language, psychology, and sports science. This team should include a subject matter specialist to ensure the accurate representation of psychological constructs. The first step will be forward translation, where the scale will be translated from its original language (usually English) to Arabic. This process will ensure that the meaning and cultural relevance of the items are preserved.

Following this, a back-forward translation will be conducted by a different set of bilingual experts who are unfamiliar with the original scale. They will translate the Arabic version back into English to verify accuracy and consistency. The back-translated version will then be compared with the original to identify any discrepancies in meaning. Finally, an expert review will be conducted. A panel of experts will review both the forward and back translations to resolve any ambiguities and inconsistencies. The translations will then be modified as necessary to ensure that the scale remains contextually appropriate.

5.4 Adaptation phase

During the adaptation phase, cultural adaptation will be crucial. Items will be modified to reflect the cultural values and norms of Arabic-speaking athletes. Focus group discussions with athletes from different Arabic countries will be conducted to identify language barriers or cultural misinterpretations.

Psychological and language expertise will be essential in this phase. Psychological and language experts will be involved to review item clarity, relevance, and cultural sensitivity. The psychological expert will assess the validity and reliability through pilot testing, while the language expert will ensure clarity and accuracy.

Pilot testing will then be carried out with a small group of athletes, typically 20–30 participants, to assess item clarity and relevance. Qualitative feedback will be collected on items that may be confusing or culturally inappropriate.

5.5 Validation phase

In the validation phase, sample selection will be a critical first step. A diverse sample of Arabic-speaking athletes across various sports and countries will be selected, ensuring a representative distribution of age, gender, and competitive level.

Reliability testing will follow, beginning with an internal consistency analysis using Cronbach's alpha for each subscale to assess reliability. Temporal stability will also be tested through test-retest reliability, particularly for scales measuring stable constructs.

To evaluate factorial validity, Exploratory Factor Analysis (EFA) will be performed to explore the underlying structure of the scale. This will be followed by Confirmatory Factor Analysis (CFA) to confirm the hypothesized structure and assess model fit.

Construct validity will then be examined by correlating the new scale with established scales measuring similar constructs, ensuring convergent validity. Divergent validity will also be confirmed to ensure that the scale does not measure unrelated constructs.

Concurrent validity will be investigated by examining relationships between translated scale scores and relevant psychological and performance outcomes for athletes. Finally, sensitivity and specificity will be assessed using receiver operating characteristic (ROC) curve analysis to determine the scale's ability to differentiate between performance levels.

5.6 Final testing and refinement

In the final testing and refinement phase, scale items will be refined based on findings from psychometric analyses. IRT will be employed to enhance item performance and ensure cultural fit. This step will ensure that the scale is both clear and reliable.

Following refinement, a final validation study will be conducted with a larger sample to confirm the robustness of the scale across different populations and contexts. This step will help to ensure the scale's applicability in diverse settings. The findings from the validation study will then be reported and disseminated. This will include publishing the psychometric properties and providing recommendations for using the scale with Arabic-speaking athletes. Additionally, guidelines will be provided for future research and interventions that utilize the scale, ensuring the continued utility and relevance of the validated instrument.

5.7 Ongoing monitoring and adaptation

Ongoing monitoring and adaptation will be essential for maintaining the effectiveness and relevance of the scale within the evolving cultural and sports landscape of Arabic-speaking regions. Periodic assessments will be conducted to ensure the scale remains applicable and accurate. Follow-up studies will also be performed as necessary to revalidate the scale, adapting it to any changes in cultural norms or contexts.

By adhering to this methodology, researchers will be able to reliably adapt, culturally tailor, and psychometrically validate positive psychology scales for Arabic-speaking athletes. This process will facilitate the accurate assessment of key psychological constructs in sports contexts. The revised methodology will offer a comprehensive framework for researchers, contributing to a deeper understanding of athlete well-being in these cultures.

6. Conclusion

Over the past two decades, numerous scales and inventories have been developed in positive psychology, primarily based on theoretical models and knowledge frameworks from North America and Europe. Many of these research instruments were originally designed in English and subsequently translated and adapted into other languages, cultures, and contexts.

It is recommended that, for the initial phase of utilizing reliable and valid scales in different cultures (such as Arab culture), translation and adaptation be the preferred methodologies for several reasons. While acknowledging the advantages of this approach, such as establishing a knowledge base and conserving time and resources, it is emphasized the importance of adhering to a rigorous scientific methodology when adapting and validating these instruments for the Arab context. This methodology facilitates the assessment of the universality of these instruments and enables cross-cultural comparisons.

To establish a solid knowledge base, careful selection of research instruments is essential before translation and adaptation. The instruments must be suitable for the sample, culture, and other relevant factors. After verifying the psychometric properties using various methods, it is crucial to ensure that only valid and reliable scales are utilized. Therefore, a standardized methodology for translation, adaptation, and contextualization is necessary, considering specific activities (e.g., training, competition) and the characteristics of the target population. For instance, adaptation for non-elite, non-adult youth athletes requires accounting for differences compared to samples with special physical or intellectual abilities.

Moreover, the researcher notes that developing new research instruments in the Arab context can be appropriate, both for general purposes and specific contexts. Studies from Western contexts have demonstrated that research instruments can be developed for specialized domains (e.g., physical education as an internal activity, team resilience, and gym training). However, it is essential to first verify the psychometric properties of any adapted instrument before utilizing it with the main study sample.

The present work examines the emerging and specialized area of validating positive psychology scales in the sports field, with a particular emphasis on Arabic-speaking countries. It contributes to filling a gap in the existing academic literature and highlights the importance of translating, adapting, and validating scales for specific cultural contexts. The chapter includes a review of pertinent studies, discussing both progress and challenges in translating and validating scales across diverse cultural settings, especially in Arabic-speaking regions. It also presents a structured approach for the translation, adaptation, and validation of psychological scales, drawing on international methodologies. This approach offers a practical guide that can support both researchers and practitioners. By emphasizing the significance of positive psychology in sports, this chapter has the potential to impact both research and practice, particularly in regions with less-established traditions in this field, such as Arabic-speaking countries.

Finally, utilization of IRT in the adaptation and validation of positive psychology scales offers significant benefits that enhance the precision and reliability of measurement instruments and improve the overall quality of the scales.

Author details

Marei Ahmed[1,2,3]

1 Psychology Department, Humanities and Sciences College, Ajman University, UAE

2 LINP2, Université de Paris Nanterre, France

3 Council of Advisors, The International Positive Psychology Association (IPPA), USA

*Address all correspondence to: msalamayounes@hotmail.fr

References

[1] Salama-Younes M. Books: Theoretical Models and Global Research Applications: Positive Psychology in the Field of Sports. Vol. 7. Middle East Journal of Positive Psychology; 2021. Available from: https://www.middleeastjournalofpositivepsychology.org/index.php/mejpp/article/view/135

[2] Salama-Younes M. Towards a positive sport psychology: A prospective investigation in physical practice. World Journal of Sport Sciences. 2011;**4**(2):104-115

[3] Salama-Younes M. Validation of the mental health continuum short form and subjective vitality scale with Egyptian adolescent athletes. In: The Human Pursuit of Well-Being: A Cultural Approach. Croatia: Springer; 2011b. pp. 221-234. Available from: http://ovidsp.ovid.com/ovidweb.cgi?T=JS&PAGE=reference&D=psyc8&NEWS=N&AN=2011-15071-020

[4] Salama-Younes M. Positive psychology in physical education and sport sciences: Interference and interaction. Middle East Journal of Positive Psychology. 2018;**4**(1):65-79

[5] Salama-Younes M, Massoud WA. Validity and reliability of well-being scales: A study on Egyptian physically active senior-aged adults. Chronicle of Advances in Positive Health and Well-Being. 2018;**1**:8

[6] Salama-Younes M. Rasch analysis and confirmatory factor analysis for the flourishing model with masters athletes: Study from France. Assiut Journal of Sport Science and Arts. 2014;**1**:445-466

[7] Seligman ME, Csikszentmihalyi M. Positive psychology. An introduction. The American Psychologist. 2000;**55**(1):5-14

[8] Seligman MEP. Flourish: A visionary new understanding of happiness and well-being. Journal of Sport Sciences (Egypt: Simon and Schuster). 2011

[9] IPPA. 2025. Available from: https://ippanetwork.org/ [Accessed: January 13, 2025]

[10] Horn TS, Smith AL. Advances in Sport and Exercise Psychology. 4th ed. Human Kinetics; 2018

[11] Brady A, Grenville-Cleave B. Positive Psychology in Sport and Physical Activity: An Introduction. India: Routledge; 2017

[12] Salama-Younes M, Hashim M. Passion, vitality and life satisfaction for physically active old adults. Journal of Positive Psychology. 2018;**13**(3):309-319

[13] Ali ME, Salama-Younes M. Flourishing, vitality and life satisfaction for Egyptian male judo players. Indian Journal of Positive Psychology. 2021;**12**(1):1-6

[14] Santi G, Williams T, Mellalieu SD, Wadey R, Carraro A. The athlete psychological well-being inventory: Factor equivalence with the sport injury-related growth inventory. Psychology of Sport and Exercise. 2024;**74**:102656

[15] Nogueira López A, Márquez Rosa S, del Salguero Valle A, Aranzana Juarros M, Molinero González O. Psychometric properties of the spanish version of the short grit scale-running (grit-sr). Revista Internacional de Medicina y Ciencias de la Actividad

Física y del Deporte. 2023;**23**(93):19. ISSN-e 1577-0354

[16] Fung SF. Evaluating the psychometric properties of the gratitude questionnaire in a Chinese sample: Comparing the 6-item and 5-item versions. Mindfulness. 2024;**15**(9):2321-2329

[17] Borrajo E, Azanza G, Urquijo I. An adaptation of the psychological capital questionnaire for the sports environment. Revista de Psicología del Deporte (Journal of Sport Psychology). 2022;**31**(4):176-185

[18] Pereira da Silva MP, de Campos D, Franco Pereira LS, Peixoto EM. Investigation of the psychometric properties of the self-compassion scale in young athletes. Revista Iberoamericana De Diagnostico Y Evaluacion-E Avaliacao Psicologica. 2022;**3**(64):157-170

[19] Sood S, Puri D. Psychological capital and positive mental health of student-athletes: Psychometric properties of the sport psychological capital questionnaire. Current Psychology. 2023;**42**(25):21759-21774

[20] Peixoto EM, Nakano TDC, Castillo RA, Oliveira LP, Balbinotti MAA. Passion scale: Psychometric properties and factorial invariance via exploratory structural equation modeling (ESEM). Paidéia (Ribeirão Preto). 2019;**29**:e2911

[21] Lichtenstein MB, Jensen ES, Larsen PV, Omdahl MK, Szabo A. Passion for exercise has three dimensions: Psychometric evaluation of the passion scale in a Danish fitness sample. Translational Sports Medicine. 2020;**3**(6):638-648

[22] do Nascimento Junior JRA, de Fortes LS, Freire GLM, de Oliveira DV, Fiorese L, Cronin LD. Cross-cultural adaptation and psychometric properties of the Portuguese version of the life skills scale for sport. Measurement in Physical Education and Exercise Science. 2020;**24**(1):11-24

[23] Bicalho CCF, de Melo GF, Noce F. Evidence of validity and perspectives for resilience scales in sport. Psicologia: Teoria e Pesquisa. 2022;**38**:e38214. Available from: https://www.scielo.br/j/ptp/a/mm6tjtJSRy4dc6mFxkSmhzd/

[24] Salama-Younes M. Initial validation of the Arabic version of the psychological flourishing scale with Egyptian athletes students. Assiut Journal of Sport Science and Arts. 2014;**1**:574-594

[25] Salama-Younes M. Subjective vitality is a mediator in the relationships between harmonious, obsessive passion and life satisfaction for physically active old adults. The International Scientific Journal of Physical Education and Sport Sciences. 2015;**1**(1):76-86

[26] Salama-Younes M. Psychometric properties of the psychological flourishing scale in an Egyptian setting. Journal of Psychology in Africa. 2017;**27**(4):310-315

[27] Abbassi M, Abbassi W, Fenouillet F, Naceur A, Abbassi M, Abbassi W, et al. Validation of the flow scale related to physical education in Arabic language. Advances in Physical Education. 2021;**11**(2):246-260

[28] Mnadla S, Elloumi A, Hajji J, Bragazzi NL. Psychometric data concerning the positive and negative affect schedule – Direction (PANAS-D) in athletes in Arabic-Tunisian language supporting a 2-factor structure of its short modified version. Data in Brief. 2017;**11**:301

[29] Ben Salha M, Kern L, Abdelatif F, Nabli EH, Baria A, Fournier JF. Adaptation and Validation of the Arabic Version of the Mindfulness Inventory for Sport. 2022;**129**(6):1838-1852. DOI: 10.1177/00315125221127513

[30] Ahmed M, Abdelrahman RM, Benlahcene A. Passion types and life satisfaction among older adult Moroccans: Reliability of scores and mediation by resilience. Journal of Psychology in Africa. 2024;**34**(1):19-25

[31] Vallerand RJ, Halliwell WR. A methodology of trans-cultural validation of psychological questionnaires: Implications for sports psychology. Canadian Journal of Applied Sport Sciences. Journal Canadien des Sciences Appliquees Au Sport. 1983;**8**(1):9-18

[32] Cruchinho P, López-Franco MD, Capelas ML, Almeida S, Bennett PM, Miranda da Silva M, et al. Translation, cross-cultural adaptation, and validation of measurement instruments: A practical guideline for novice researchers. Journal of Multidisciplinary Healthcare. 2024;**1**:2701-2728

Chapter 6

Psychometric Analysis of an Instrument to Study Retention in Engineering: Do Results Support the Gender Similarity Hypothesis?

Kenneth J. Reid

Abstract

Incoming engineering programs are typically highly qualified students with strong academic credentials. However, retention in engineering remains lower than most other programs of study. Efforts to address retention by modeling student success, and incorporating noncognitive attributes into those models has proven somewhat successful, and inclusion of affective characteristics have proven to be more accurate than those using only cognitive variables. The Student Attitudinal Success Instrument (SASI-I), a survey assessing nine specific noncognitive constructs, was developed based largely on existing, validated instruments. It was designed to collect data on affective (non-cognitive) characteristics for incoming engineering students (a) which can be collected prior to the first year and (b) for which higher education institutions may have an influence during students' first year of study. Three years of data from incoming first-year engineering students were collected and analyzed. This work was conducted toward investigating the following research questions: 1. Do the scale scores of the instrument demonstrate evidence of reliability and validity, and what is the normative taxonomy of the scale scores of first-year engineering students across multiple years? 2. How similar or dissimilar are the normative taxonomies of male vs. female students, and do these taxonomies support the Gender Similarity Hypothesis? 3. Does evidence suggest a trend over time in the difference for characteristics where differences between male and female students were found? Support for the gender similarity hypothesis was found. Differences in almost all affective characteristics between genders were found to be insignificant with a low effect size.

Keywords: affective, cluster analysis, engineering, gender, non-cognitive, normative taxonomy, retention, SASI-I

1. Introduction

Students admitted into engineering programs are largely academically talented, with high strong grade point averages and standardized exam scores above the norm. Unfortunately, many of these students fail to complete their engineering degree, often leaving at the end of their first year of study. Further, the unwieldy prerequisite structure in engineering makes it difficult for students to transfer *into* engineering, which means that engineering programs show a significantly lower percentage of retained students when compared to other disciplines.

There is a significant body of literature in retention in undergraduates, including retention within Science, Technology, Engineering and Mathematics (STEM) and within engineering. Efforts to address lower retention, especially among under-represented students, including females, have been well documented. These include the development of first-year engineering programs, to pedagogical improvements, to curricula focused on design, mentorship programs, experiential curricula, etc. Studies have demonstrated evidence of strong predictive power of noncognitive attitudes over purely cognitive measures of students in retention and future academic performance [1–12].

One of the initial surveys designed specifically to address noncognitive attributes that may be assessed prior to the start of the student's first year and for which interventions may be developed is the Student Attitudinal Success Inventory (SASI-I). This paper focuses on the psychometric analysis of the initial version of the SASI-I, which was shown to be valid and reliable, and further discusses the use of normative taxonomy of first-year engineering students across multiple years to assess engineering students' multifaceted non-cognitive attributes. Further, studies of shifts in noncognitive attributes over the first year of study have repeatedly shown trends for affective characteristics in an unfavorable direction [8, 13, 14]. The scale was used to examine differences by gender, and whether the data supports the Gender Similarity Hypothesis. This paper introduces analysis techniques in the study of noncognitive characteristics of first year engineering students.

2. Driving research questions

Specific research questions which led to this analysis include:

1. What is the evidence of reliability and validity for the SASI-I instrument consisting of a number of affective/attitudinal factors related to student success, based on incoming first-year engineering student responses?

2. How similar or dissimilar are the normative taxonomies of male vs. female students, and do these taxonomies support the Gender Similarity Hypothesis?

3. Does evidence suggest a trend of increase or decrease over time in the difference for characteristics where differences between male and female students were found?

3. Instrumentation

Data were based on three incoming cohorts of undergraduate students enrolling in engineering in a large Midwestern university over a three-year period: cohort 1 (2004, N = 1605), cohort 2 (2005, *N* = 1777), and cohort 3 (2006, *N* = 1779) as shown in **Table 1**. Each cohort consists of all entering first-year students who were admitted to the college of engineering but had not yet started their first semester. A small number of included students did not enroll or attend classes at the institution.

Data on the affective and attitudinal characteristics of all incoming engineering students were gathered using the 161-item SASI-I. This data was utilized to identify the normative taxonomy of incoming student cohorts [15]. Students completed the SASI-I online as part of a mandatory orientation activity, providing responses on a Likert scale ranging from 1 (Strongly Agree) to 5 (Strongly Disagree). The SASI-I was administered alongside placement tests (e.g., math, chemistry) before the first semester and again at the end of the academic year. Students who did not complete all three components of the SASI-I assessment were excluded from the analysis. The self-report measures were designed to evaluate students' affective and attitudinal beliefs across various constructs, each identified in the literature as critical to academic success [1, 15].

- *Academic motivation*:
  - 25 items in four subfactors: Control, Challenge, Curiosity and Career.
- *Metacognition*:
  - 20 items in four subfactors: Planning, Self-monitoring/Self-Checking, Cognitive Strategy and Awareness.
- *Deep learning*:
  - 10 items in two subfactors, Motive and Strategy.
- *Surface learning*:
  - 10 items, originally with identical subfactors to Deep Learning. Factor analysis yielded two different subfactors, labeled Memorization and Studying.
- *Academic self-efficacy*:
  - 10 individual items that proved to not form specific subfactors.
- *Leadership*:
  - 20 items with four subfactors, Motivation, Planning, Self-Assessment and Teammates.

	Pre-year			Post-year		
	Number	**Male**	**Female**	**Number**	**Male**	**Female**
Cohort 1	1605	1297 (80.8%)	308 (19.2%)	722	563 (78.0%)	159 (22.0%)
Cohort 2	1777	1502 (84.2%)	275 (15.5%)	627	516 (82.3%)	111 (17.7%)
Cohort 3	1779	1482 (83.3%)	297 (16.7%)			

Table 1.
Demographics of student cohort groups, pre- and post-surveys.

- *Team vs. individual orientation*:
    - o 10 items in two subfactors, Individual and Team Dynamic.
- *Expectancy-value*:
    - o 32 items in five subfactors: Academic Resources, Community Involvement, Employment Opportunities, Persistence and Social Engagement.
- *Major Decision*:
    - o 21 items in four subfactors: Certainty of Decision, Difficulty in Decision, Personal Issues, and Urgency. One question was shown not to load to any of the subfactors and is assessed on its own (ironically, Independence).

The multilevel structure allows each item to load onto both a higher-order construct or general factor (e.g., Major Decision) and a specific subfactor within the construct's domain (e.g., the Certainty of Decision subfactor under Major Decision), enabling analysis at various levels.

Table 2 shows a summary of constructs, subconstructs, and number of items in each construct and subconstruct.

Construct	**Origin**	N_S	N_t	**Subconstruct**	N_i
Intrinsic motivation	Academic Intrinsic Motivation Scale (AIMS) [16]	4	25	Career	5
				Challenge	6
				Control	7
				Curiosity	7
Academic self-efficacy	Based on [17]	1	10	Self-efficacy	10
Expectancy-value	Based on [18]	5	32	Expected use, acad resources	5
				Community involvement	4
				Employment opportunities	8
				Persistence	7
				Social engagement	8
Deep learning approach	Revised two-factor Study Process Questionnaire (R-SPQ-2F) [19]	2	10	Motive	5
				Strategy	5
Surface learning approach		2	10	Memorization	3
				Studying	7
Metacognition	Based on State Metacognitive Inventory [20]	4	20	Awareness	5
				Cognitive strategy	5
				Planning	5
				Self-checking	5

Construct	Origin	N_S	N_t	Subconstruct	N_i
Leadership	Based on [21]	4	23	Motivation	5
				Planning	4
				Self-assessment	7
				Teammates	7
Team vs. individual orientation	Based on [22]	2	10	Individual dynamic	5
				Team dynamic	5
Major decision	Based on [23]	5	21	Certainty of decision	3
				Difficulty of decision	10
				Personal issues	4
				Urgency	3
				Independence	1
Total	*9 constructs*	29	161		161

Table 2.
Constructs, subconstructs, and number of items in each construct.

4. Psychometric analysis

4.1 Internal consistency of scales and subscales

Internal consistency of scale and subscale scores was shown by calculating Cronbach's coefficient alpha; values exceeding 0.80 are desired [24, 25]. The Spearman-Brown formula [26, 27] was used to estimate Cronbach's alpha in any subscale containing less than 10 items since Cronbach's coefficient alpha is sensitive to the number of items within a construct.

4.2 Construct and subscale structure

Factor analytic procedures were employed to examine the multidimensional structures of the scales. Each item was designed to load onto a general construct (e.g., Surface Learning) and a specific subscale within the construct's domain (e.g., the Studying subscale under Surface Learning). This approach reflects the multidimensional nature of the scales. Constructs with a pre-defined structure were analyzed using Confirmatory Factor Analysis (CFA), while Exploratory Factor Analysis (EFA) was applied to constructs developed specifically for this instrument to establish their subscale structures.

EFA was conducted using SAS (version 9.1.3) with the proc. factor procedure and a promax rotation. Promax rotation optimizes the alignment of axes to achieve the best item loadings. The appropriate number of factors was determined using the Kaiser criterion, which identifies factors with eigenvalues greater than 1, and by analyzing the scree plot of eigenvalues. These methods ensured a robust foundation for defining the factor structure of the scales.

CFA was then performed to test the factor structure of each construct. Fit was assessed from the 2004 student cohort using LISREL™. Path diagrams were developed to specify the relationship between each latent variable and its associated subscale, excluding *self-efficacy*. The null hypothesis (H_0) is that the data will adequately fit the proposed structure for each construct at the item level. For constructs requiring EFA to define subscales, a randomly selected subset of the data (n = 500) was used for EFA, while a mutually exclusive subset (n = 1000) was used to validate the structure through CFA. This two-stage approach ensured both exploration and confirmation of the factor structures.

Model fit in CFA was evaluated using multiple criteria, including the chi-square statistic, Comparative Fit Index (CFI), Goodness of Fit Index (GFI), and Root Mean Square Error of Approximation (RMSEA). Although the chi-square statistic was reported, its sensitivity to large sample sizes (e.g., >1500 students) limits its applicability as a sole indicator. Fit was assessed using thresholds proposed by Hu and Bentler [28], where CFI > 0.95 and RMSEA < 0.08 indicate acceptable fit, with RMSEA < 0.05 suggesting excellent fit. Tanguma [29] also noted that the CFI and GFI were stable with large samples (n > 500), with GFI > 0.90 representing acceptable model fit.

4.3 Cohort group normative taxonomy

To show factor stability over time, McDermott's [30] three stage cluster analysis clusters students with similar response patterns. This was used on each cohort to determine normative taxonomies. Each cohort was compared to each other cohort to determine similarity from year to year.

The first step of the analysis was to convert raw scores to normalized z-scores to equally weight each of the nine affective/attitudinal constructs with respect to each other. Mutually exclusive groups of approximately equal size partitions of the data using Ward's minimum variance method (*B* = number of blocks) [31]. For example, data for the 2005 cohort consists of nine blocks: seven with 197 and two with 199 students, with a normalized z-score for each affective/attitudinal construct for each student. For each random block, criteria for determining the optimal number of clusters (*K*) included the R^2 statistic (the proportion of the variance accounted for by the clusters), the pseudo-F statistic over the pseudo-t^2 statistic [32] and Mojina's first stopping rule [33].

The second stage involved formation of a $(B \bullet K)$ x $(B \bullet K)$ similarity matrix reflecting the consequence of merging any two clusters. Each resulting cluster was considered as input to the cluster analysis procedure, resulting in the final number of clusters indicated for the complete data set. The resulting homogeneity coefficients indicate, in this case, the consistency from year to year for each cohort group.

Finally, the third stage applied k-means iterative (nonhierarchical) partitioning to relocate potentially misassigned individual cases to improve homogeneity coefficients. The profile of each individual is examined to ensure membership in the ideal cluster: misassigned profiles are reassigned to a profile more closely matching the individual. All analysis was done in SAS with modifications to code developed by Paul McDermott [30].

Final clusters were expected to satisfy an average within-cluster homogeneity coefficient $\bar{H} > 0.6$ [34]. Cattell's Cluster Similarity Coefficient, r_p, [35] was calculated to demonstrate cluster similarity between clusters within and between cohort groups. Higher coefficient values demonstrate better congruence: excellent similarity is shown with values greater than 0.95 while values between −0.7 and +0.7 show poor factor similarity [36].

4.4 Effect size: Cohen's *d*

Statistical significance of differences is influenced by large sample sizes, and a statistically significant difference does not *necessarily* imply a meaningful or important difference – only that a true difference of means most likely exists. Very small differences tend to become significant as the size of the population under study increases. The effect size, or Cohen's d, is a measure of the effect or the importance of the difference [36–38]. Cohen's d is found:

$$d = \frac{M_1 - M_2}{\sigma_{pooled}} \tag{1}$$

where M_1 and M_2 are the means of the male and female population. The pooled standard deviation, σ_{pooled}, is the root-mean-square of the standard deviations of the two populations [36]. That is:

$$\sigma_{pooled} = \frac{\sqrt{\sigma_1^2 + \sigma_2^2}}{2} \tag{2}$$

Hyde [39, 40] defined and named ranges for effect sizes as part of the Gender Similarity Hypothesis as:

- near-zero, $d \leq 0.10$
- small, $0.11 < d \leq 0.35$
- moderate, $0.36 < d \leq 0.65$
- large, $0.66 < d \leq 1.0$, and
- very large, $d > 1.0$.

5. Results

5.1 Structure of the overall instrument

Exploratory Factor Analysis (EFA) was used to verify the predefined structure from the literature for Motivation, Metacognition, and Deep Learning. EFA results did not agree with the existing structure for Surface Learning, leading to a reexamination of the factors. Academic Self-efficacy, Leadership, Team vs. Individual Orientation, Expectancy-Value and Major Decision did not have a defined structure, so EFA was used to define the subfactors. Fit indices including chi-square, GFI, RMSEA and CFI for each construct are shown in **Table 3**.

Motivation, Metacognition and Deep Learning constructs: Subscales for motivation, metacognition and deep learning were unchanged from those originally presented in their literature. Factor analysis supported the subscales as originally specified. CFA results show an acceptable fit for each of these constructs with values for GFI > 0.9, CFI > 0.9 and RMSEA <0.08.

Surface Learning: The subscales of surface learning were originally defined as *Motive* and *Strategy*, the same as those of deep learning. EFA indicated that the subscale *Strategy* itself loaded into two separate factors which is not indicative of a homogeneous construct. EFA results on the entire Surface Learning construct showed

	χ^2	χ^2 df	$pr > \chi2$	GFI	RMSEA	CFI
Motivation	902.6	240	<.0001	0.99	0.053	1.00
Metacognition	767.53	141	<.0001	0.99	0.067	1.00
Leadership	522.16	197	<.0001	0.99	0.041	1.00
Team vs. Individual Orientation	63.45	22	<.0001	1.00	0.012	1.00
Expectancy Value	1410.1	417	<.0001	0.98	0.049	1.00
Major Decision	805.16	153	<.0001	0.99	0.065	1.00
Deep Learning	49.73	22	.00064	1.00	0.036	1.00
Surface Learning (original subscales)	152.5	25	<.0001	0.97	0.072	0.942
Surface Learning (revised)	31.34	24	0.14	0.99	0.013	1.00
Academic Self-Efficacy			n/a			

Surface Learning original and revised are listed to show improvement with revision of subscale structure; χ^2 = Chi-squared; χ^2 df = Chi-square degrees of freedom; GFI = Goodness of Fit Index; RMSEA = Root Mean Square Error of Approximation estimate; CFI = Bentley's Comparative Fit Index.

Table 3.
Confirmatory factor analysis results for each construct.

items clearly loading into two factors, which were named *Memorization* and *Studying* based on context of the questions. CFA results indicated a significant improvement in fit. The redefined structure with modified subscales resulted in a value of chi-square that was not significant, meaning that the data did indeed fit the theoretical structure, even given the very large sample size.

Leadership, Team vs. Individual Orientation, and Expectancy-Value: Subscales for each of these constructs were defined based on exploratory factor analysis on a subset of the data: results were validated using CFA on a mutually exclusive subset of the data. **Table 3** shows the results of the CFA for each construct, with values for GFI > 0.9, CFI > 0.9 and RMSEA < 0.05, verifying the validity of the structure for each construct.

Major Decision: Results of the EFA showed the items in the Major Decision construct loaded to five subscales and CFA results showed an acceptable fit for this structure (GFI = 0.99, CFI > 0.99 and RMSEA = 0.065). The Major Decision scale contained one question which was shown not to load on any particular subscale and is presented independent of the subscales (ironically, named *Independence*). Three items were shown to negatively correlate to the remainder of the scale, and were reverse scored during the analysis.

Academic Self-Efficacy: EFA performed on the academic self-efficacy construct indicated no subscales.

5.2 Internal consistency of scales and subscales

Reliability of the instrument is demonstrated with acceptable values of Cronbach's alpha for each construct and subscale for each cohort [24, 25, 41]. Complete results are shown in **Table 4**. Values of Cronbach's alpha are shown after reverse-scoring two of the items in the Major Decision scale.

Cronbach's coefficient alpha values for all scales exceed 0.8 with two exceptions: Surface learning ($\alpha = 0.79$) and Team vs. Individual Orientation ($\alpha \geq 0.75$), demonstrating the homogeneous nature of each construct [25, 42]. The lack of variation in values of Cronbach's coefficient alpha for different populations, in this case different student cohort groups, is one indication of stability and repeatability of the scales over time.

Number of items		Cohort 1	Cohort 2	Cohort 3
Motivation	25	**0.93**	**0.93**	**0.93**
Career	5	0.82	0.81	0.83
Challenge	6	0.80	0.79	0.80
Control	7	0.79	0.80	0.79
Curiosity	7	0.81	0.81	0.82
Metacognition	20	0.92	0.92	0.93
Awareness	5	0.77	0.79	0.79
Cognitive Strategy	5	0.78	0.79	0.79
Planning	5	0.76	0.78	0.79
Self-Checking	5	0.72	0.74	0.76
Deep Learning	10	0.81	0.83	0.82
Motive	5	0.69	0.70	0.69
Strategy	5	0.67	0.71	0.71
Surface Learning	10	0.79	0.79	0.79
Memorization	3	0.60	0.59*	0.62
Studying	7	0.80	0.79	0.80
Leadership	23	0.89	0.89	0.89
Motivation	5	0.69	0.69	0.69
Planning	4	0.70	0.70	0.67
Self-assessment	7	0.78	0.77	0.77
Teammates	7	0.68	0.70	0.68
Team vs. Individual Orientation	10	0.75	0.79	0.76
individual	5	0.61	0.63	0.59*
team dynamic	5	0.69	0.74	0.73
Expectancy Value	32	0.90	0.91	0.91
Academic Resources	5	0.75	0.76	0.76
Community Involvement	4	0.71	0.72	0.72
Employment opportunities	8	0.81	0.82	0.82
Persistence	7	0.80	0.81	0.81
Social Engagement	8	0.81	0.80	0.80
Major Decision	21	0.85	0.85	0.85
Certainty of decision	3	0.49*	0.49*	0.53*
Difficulty in decision	10	0.92	0.92	0.92
Personal issues	4	0.60	0.61	0.56*
Urgency	3	0.57*	0.58*	0.59*
Independence	1	—	—	—
Academic Self-Efficacy	10	0.90	0.90	0.90

Alpha values less than 0.6.

Table 4.
Values of Cronbach's coefficient alpha for each construct and subscale.

In cases where there were fewer than 10 items in a subscale, the Spearman-Brown formula was used to assess values of Cronbach's coefficient alpha for a consistent number of items. Using the Spearman-Brown formula [26, 27, 43] results in an estimate for Cronbach's coefficient alpha for a construct when interpolated to a specified number of items. Some subscales with very few items were outside of this range; the small number of items within each subscale certainly contribute to low values of alpha. In each case, values of alpha were consistent from cohort to cohort, further demonstrating the internal consistency of the constructs and subscales.

5.3 Cluster analysis: Pre-year survey

McDermott's three stage cluster analysis was used to derive the core profiles for each of the 3 years of cohort data from cohort 1 to cohort 3. The primary goal of this analysis was to identify normative taxonomies of individuals who exhibit similar profiles within a given cluster, yet dissimilar profiles across clusters. Similar taxonomies are indicated by a consistent number of core profiles, and profiles of similar magnitude and shape as determined by the cluster homogeneity coefficient $\bar{H} > 0.6$ [34] and Cattell's similarity coefficient [35] (similar: $r_p > 0.95$, dissimilar: $|r_p| < 0.7$) [44].

Cluster analysis resulted in three core profiles for each cohort. The shape and pattern of each profile was consistent from cohort to cohort, showing strong repeatability and stability.

Figure 1 shows an overlay of plots of the means of each construct for each cluster of students. Specific constructs are shown on the x-axis, with center values (normalized z-scores) for each construct for each cluster on the y-axis. There is no significance to the order of the constructs on the x-axis. Center means for each core cluster within each cohort are shown in **Table 5**. Three distinct clusters, and the shape of

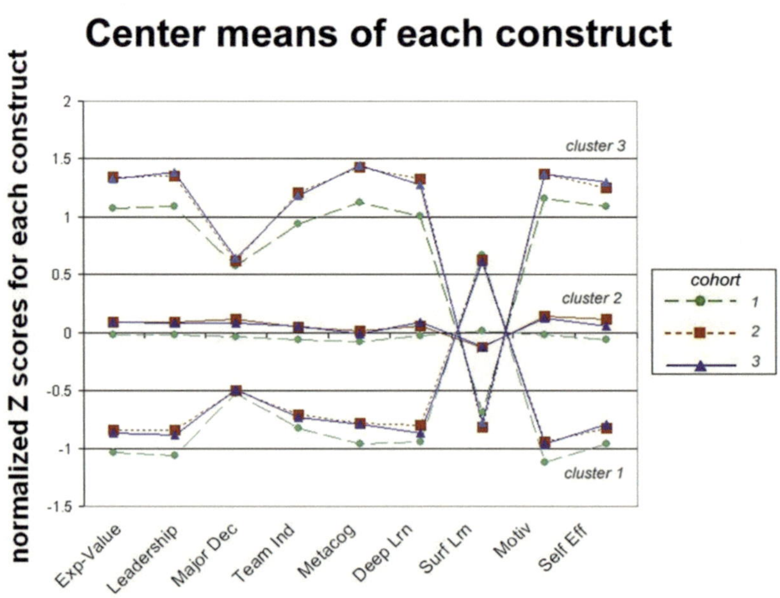

Figure 1.
Overlay of plots of normalized center means for each construct, shown for each cohort of students. Data points are shown as connected to illustrate similarly/dissimilarity of each cluster, and are not meant to imply a relationship between constructs.

Cluster	Cohort	$Z_{ex\text{-}val}$	Z_{lead}	$Z_{maj\ dec}$	Z_{team}	Z_{meta}	Z_{deep}	Z_{surf}	Z_{motiv}	Z_{self}	n
	2004	-1.03	-1.06	-0.52	-0.83	-0.96	-0.94	0.67	-1.12	-0.96	400
1	2005	-0.85	-0.85	-0.50	-0.71	-0.78	-0.80	0.63	-0.94	-0.83	611
(Lower)	2006	-0.87	-0.89	-0.49	-0.73	-0.79	-0.87	0.61	-0.96	-0.79	570
	2004	-0.02	-0.02	-0.03	-0.06	-0.08	-0.03	0.02	-0.02	-0.06	804
2	2005	0.09	0.09	0.12	0.05	0.01	0.06	-0.13	0.14	0.11	840
(Middle)	2006	0.09	0.08	0.08	0.06	-0.01	0.09	-0.12	0.13	0.05	892
	2004	1.07	1.09	0.58	0.94	1.12	1.01	-0.69	1.16	1.09	401
3	2005	1.35	1.35	0.62	1.21	1.43	1.33	-0.82	1.37	1.25	326
(upper)	2006	1.33	1.39	0.65	1.19	1.45	1.28	-0.78	1.37	1.30	317

Table 5.
Center means for each construct for core cluster.

each cluster of students, are both significant. Students who tended to rate themselves at least one standard deviation stronger than other students tended to do so across the board for all constructs with the exception of surface learning: the sharp spike seen in the plots indicates these students view their learning style as deep (developing an understanding and appreciation of material) as opposed to surface (memorization). As might be expected, those students rating themselves below the affective/attitudinal norms indicated a propensity toward surface learning. Students in cluster 1 responded approximately one standard deviation below the norm (with the exception of Surface Learning) while students in cluster 3 responded one standard deviation above the average (again, with the exception of Surface Learning). Students in cluster 2 clustered about the norms for each construct. There is no significance to the cluster numbers; they are used only to distinguish between groups.

Table 6 shows the number of students within each profile. Final clusters satisfied an average within cluster homogeneity coefficient $\bar{H} > 0.99$ (**Table 6**), demonstrating that the clusters were indeed homogeneous. The plots in **Figure 2** show year to year consistency in shape with minimal variation in values for each construct. Stability is demonstrated with minimal variability in the center values for each cohort over multiple years.

Cattell's Cluster Similarity Coefficients were calculated to objectively determine the similarity between each cluster for each year. Excellent cluster similarity is demonstrated with values of Cattell's coefficient $r_p > 0.95$; values of Cattell's coefficient comparing clusters expected to be highly similar are consistently $0.94 < r_p < 1.00$ (see **Table 7**), demonstrating these clusters to be similar and stable over this time period. Clusters expected to be dissimilar show comparison values well below values indicating similarity, demonstrating these clusters to be dissimilar to each other. Strong coefficients of similarity and similar percentages of students within each cluster show that student responses tend to remain stable from year to year.

Interestingly, the smallest spread among cohorts was found in Major Decision, indicating that students in each profile appear to differ *least* in their initial intent to pursue an engineering degree. The widest disparities between clusters appear to be among motivation and metacognition; this may be expected given the strong academic backgrounds of incoming engineering students.

6. Differences by gender

Engineering programs in the United States continue to see exceptionally low female enrollment. While other majors with historically predominant male enrollment have seen an increase in the percentage of female students, the percentage within engineering has remained low, with females accounting for about 20% of engineering graduates compared to about 50% of graduates in medicine and law [45]. Retention rates for male and female students are comparable: in its report "Educating the Engineer of 2020", the National Academies states, "Only 40 to 60 percent of entering engineering students persist to an engineering degree, and women and minorities are at the low end of that range" [46]. Are there differences in high school that can account for the discrepancy? Examination of the difference in mathematical achievement from 1974 to 1990, as more girls began taking advanced math and science courses, showed a small difference ($d = 0.14$) in performance [47]. Measuring this gap in 2008 showed no difference ($d = 0.0065$) between males and females using data from the National Assessment of Educational Progress (NAEP). Examination of

	n (2004)	$\bar{H}$ (2004)	*n* (2005)	$\bar{H}$ (2005)	*n* (2006)	$\bar{H}$ (2006)
Cluster 1 (lower)	400 (25%)	0.997	611 (35%)	0.997	570 (32%)	0.997
Cluster 2 (middle)	804 (50%)	0.998	840 (47%)	0.998	892 (50%)	0.998
Cluster 3 (upper)	401 (30%)	0.997	326 (18%)	0.997	317 (18%)	0.997

Table 6.
Number of students (n) and average within cluster homogeneity coefficient ($\bar{H}$) in each cluster for cohorts 1–3 (2004–2006).

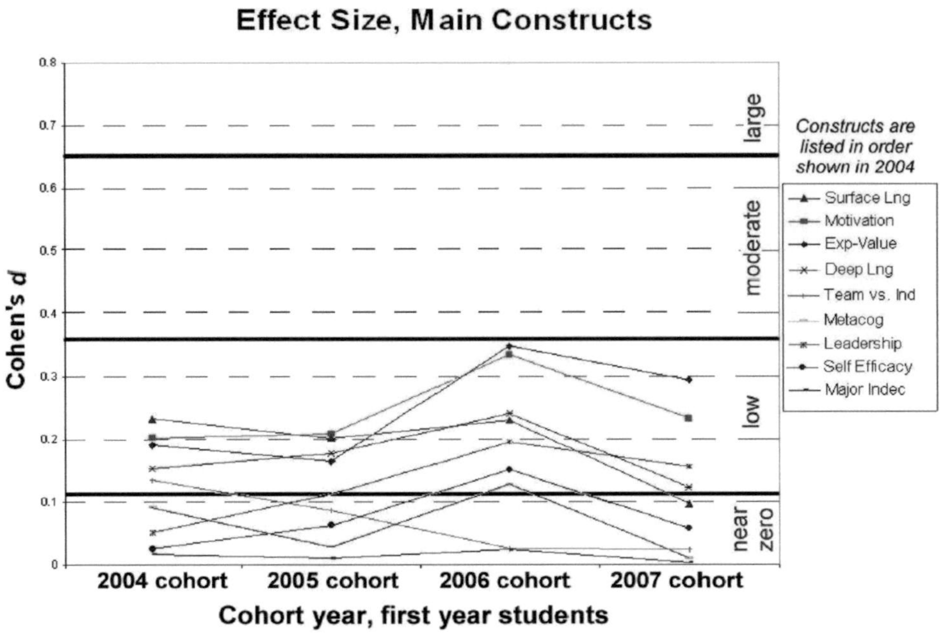

Figure 2.
Magnitude of effect sizes of male/female differences in means (Cohen's d) for each construct for each cohort.

questions requiring higher reasoning showed no difference between male and female students when analyzed [48].

Numerous studies report data showing that differences in cognitive abilities between female and male students as measured by standardized test scores, grade point averages or number of semesters of courses in major subjects are small to non-existent. Female and male students entering engineering are generally academically strong students. Following is an examination of differences between male and female students admitted to, and before entering, engineering.

6.1 Gender similarity hypothesis: The importance of effect size

Hyde [40] developed the Gender Similarities Hypothesis which theorizes that most psychological differences between male and female students are small to close to zero, and where statistically significant differences are reported, they are generally due to very large sample sizes. Specifically, as measured in terms of effect sizes, most differences are near-zero ($d \leq 0.10$) or small ($0.11 < d \leq 0.35$) as opposed to moderate ($0.36 < d \leq 0.65$) to large or very large ($d > 0.66$). Hyde's meta-analyses of literature reporting differences (or lack of differences) between sexes categorized differences between the sexes into six general areas: cognitive variables, verbal and nonverbal communication, social or personality variables, measures of psychological well-being, motor behaviors and miscellaneous. Hyde found 124 usable effect sizes between males and females and found that 78% of these are small (59) or close to zero (37). These measures vary widely and include those that are theorized to possibly be predictive of academic success (for example, self-efficacy) as well as many variables that are not theorized to be applicable to student success (for example, physical characteristics such as throwing ability).

Cluster		2005			Cluster		2006			Cluster		2006		
		1	2	3			1	2	3			1	2	3
2004	1	**0.98**	0.54	0.08	**2004**	1	**0.99**	0.53	0.08	**2005**	1	**1.00**	0.41	0.18
	2	0.29	**0.98**	−.42		2	0.30	**0.98**	−.42		2	0.44	**1.00**	−.36
	3	0.39	−.25	**0.94**		3	0.37	−.26	**0.94**		3	0.17	−.37	**1.00**

Values show the coefficient for the cluster in the year indicated for each row/column. Bold values show comparison of clusters theoretically similar.

Table 7.
Cattell's cluster similarity coefficient for each cluster 2004–2006.

Among characteristics important to success in engineering are measures of mathematical ability [46]. Hyde investigated mathematical ability in grades K-12 and found no difference in mathematical computation ability between male and female students in high school, but a small (d = 0.29) difference in complex problem solving favoring male students in the 2005 study based on data from the 1990s. In a 2008 study, Hyde showed that the effect size of the difference decreased as the number of female students taking advanced mathematics in high school grew through the 1990s and 2000s. A study of state mathematics assessments in 10 states (N > 7 million students) showed no difference between male and female students. Effect sizes for students in 10th (N > 600,000) and 11th (N > 400,000) grades were d = 0.04 and d = 0.06 respectively, both near-zero. Further analysis of the data showed a effect size of d = 0.07 for the most complex problems on the included state assessments, representing items coded as requiring greatest depth of knowledge.

In a study of differences in science performance, Hyde [39] discusses results published by the National Assessment of Educational Progress (NAEP) report [49], which show a statistically significant difference in science performance. However, because smaller differences tend to become significant as the sample size increases, this statistical significance can be attributed to the large sample size (N ≈ 100,000 per grade level). The difference in scores for 12th graders was found to be significant between male students (average science score = 149.01) and female students (average science score = 145.15). However, the effect size, d = 0.11, shows that, although the difference is significant, the magnitude of its importance is small, thus the study shows only a small difference in performance between male and female students.

6.2 Cohort group normative taxonomy

Cluster analysis was used to establish the normative taxonomy of both male and female students taken in aggregate for each cohort. Male and female taxonomies were compared to each other based on number of clusters, shape and using Cattell's similarity coefficient [35], a measure of cluster similarity. Clusters are defined by converting raw scores for each of the nine noncognitive constructs to normalized z scores; this gives equal weight to each of the nine noncognitive constructs with respect to each other. McDermott's three stage cluster analysis [30] was used separately on each cohort to determine normative taxonomies of students, clustering students with similar response patterns.

The first stage involves cluster analysis on separate mutually exclusive partitions of equal size (B = number of blocks) of the data using Ward's minimum variance method. Ideal block sizes range from 150 to 200 students. In this case, the population of male students (N = 5644) was sorted by a random number then divided into four mutually exclusive partitions. The resulting four blocks of male students and a block of female students (N = 1228) were divided into 8 or 9 blocks of 153 to 199 students each. McDermott's method proceeds by determining an optimal number of clusters (K) for each data set: criteria used to determine the number of clusters included the R^2 statistic (indicating the proportion of the variance accounted for by the clusters), the pseudo-F statistic over the pseudo-t^2 statistic [32] and Mojina's first stopping rule [33]. In this case, each separate block for male and female students resulted in three clusters.

The second stage involves formation of a (B•K) x (B•K) similarity matrix reflecting the consequence of merging any two individual clusters. Each resulting cluster is considered as input to the cluster analysis procedure, resulting in the final number of clusters indicated for the complete data set.

Finally, the third stage applies k-means iterative (nonhierarchical) partitioning to improve homogeneity coefficients by realigning individual cases. The profile membership of each individual is examined to ensure membership in the ideal cluster: misassigned individuals are reassigned to a profile more closely matching, thus improving homogeneity coefficients.

Ideally, final clusters should satisfy an average within-cluster homogeneity coefficient $\bar{H} > 0.6$ [34]. Cattell's Cluster Similarity Coefficient, r_p, demonstrates cluster similarity between clusters within and between cohort groups. Higher coefficient values demonstrate better congruence: excellent similarity is shown with values greater than 0.95 while values between −0.7 and +0.7 show poorer factor similarity [44].

6.3 Participants

Student demographic data for each cohort are shown in **Table 8**. Students who did not complete all sections of the online instrument were not considered in the analysis and are not included in the demographics presented in **Table 8** (1 student in 2004, 7 in 2005, 60 in 2006 and 16 in 2007). Percentages based on sex and ethnicity were consistent within each cohort; the disproportionate number of males in the sample is typical of students entering engineering in this and similar institutions within the United States.

6.4 Statistical significance: Nonparametric estimates of *p*

Specifying the Monte Carlo approximation when calculating p values results in (a) an estimate for the exact p value and (b) upper and lower bounds on the confidence interval for p. Initial examination of the data showed that it did not meet an assumption of normality [50], therefore, the use of nonparametric tests as opposed to more straightforward two-tailed t-tests were appropriate for use in the analysis. Standard two-tailed t tests were also run to investigate the effect of incorrectly assuming a normal distribution; therefore, two values of p were obtained for comparison: were the nonparametric tests necessary given our population?

	Number of students	Gender		Race						
		Male	Female	NA	CA	AA	AP	HS	E	DNR
2004	1605	1297 (80.8%)	308 (19.2%)	0.6%	82.2%	2.6%	9.1%	2.8%		6.7%
2005	1777	1502 (84.5%)	275 (15.5%)	0.4%	74.5%	2.1%	9.3%	2.4%	3.4%	7.7%
2006	1779	1482 (83.3%)	297 (16.7%)	0.5%	76.2%	2.4%	9.2%	2.9%	2.6%	6.0%
2007	1711	1363 (79.7%)	348 (20.3%)	0.5%	71.9%	2.0%	9.5%	3.6%	4.0%	8.5%

Key (Race): NA = Native American; CA = Caucasian; AA = African American; AP = Asian Pacific Islander; HS = Hispanic; E = Other; DNR = Did not report.

Table 8.
Description of student cohort groups.

Values of p using nonparametric tests were compared to two tailed t-tests for each construct, subfactor and individual item on the data in aggregate (N = 6872); in each case, the value of p from the t-test fell within the 90% confidence interval from the nonparametric tests. Also, there were no cases where the two values of p (parametric and nonparametric) disagreed as to whether a difference was statistically significant. Therefore, although nonparametric approximations of exact p values are calculated and are presented, more complicated nonparametric tests were probably not necessary. Upon examination, our data primarily appears as a negatively skewed Gaussian distribution; this could explain the similarity between results of the two-tailed t-test and the nonparametric tests.

6.5 Differences in superordinate constructs

Table 9 shows each construct: constructs which show statistically significant differences between male and female students are indicated. Five of the nine constructs were found to have a significant difference when examining the aggregate population (2004–2007, N = 6872): these include (1) Expectancy-Value, (2) Motivation, (3) Surface Learning, (4) Deep Learning and (5) Leadership. However, the effect sizes were all small ($d < 0.35$) to near-zero ($d < 0.11$). Therefore, while there was a difference found in the responses between males and females, the *effect* of this difference – or the *importance* – was found to be minimal. These results support the Gender Similarity Hypothesis since most (or in this case, all) of the effect sizes are small.

Figure 2 shows a plot of effect size for each construct for each year, 2004–2007. Each construct showed a low to near-zero effect size when the data is taken in aggregate as well as a low to near-zero effect size for each construct in each year. **Figure 2** shows the magnitude (absolute value) of the effect sizes, indicating the difference but not the direction (not illustrating whether male or female students had a higher mean value).

Construct	Mean, M (N = 5644)	σ, M	Mean, F (N = 1228)	σ, F	M - F		p (MC)
Expectancy-Value*	3.943	0.360	3.848	0.381	−0.094	−0.254	<0.0001
Motivation*	4.186	0.391	4.087	0.420	−0.098	−0.243	<0.0001
Surface Learning*	2.393	0.476	2.486	0.523	0.092	0.185	<0.0001
Deep Learning*	3.735	0.460	3.652	0.501	−0.082	−0.171	<0.0001
Leadership*	3.959	0.368	3.910	0.377	−0.048	−0.129	0.000
Self-efficacy	4.242	0.459	4.214	0.475	−0.029	−0.061	0.142
Team vs. Individual	3.931	0.381	3.947	0.399	0.016	0.041	0.092
Major Decision	3.581	0.483	3.580	0.479	−0.001	−0.003	0.784
Metacognition	3.931	0.406	3.932	0.421	0.001	0.001	0.467

**Statistically Significant Difference, small to near-zero effect size.*

Table 9.
Mean and standard deviation, male and female students: significance and effect size.

6.6 Differences in subfactors and individual items

Examining the differences at the subfactor level shows that, while 16 of 28 subfactors had a statistically significant difference, only one of the 28 subfactors had an effect size above 'small'. The single subfactor with a moderate effect size was within the Expectancy-Value construct: the Community Involvement subfactor had an effect size of −0.36. The magnitude of this effect size, barely inside of the moderate range ($0.35 < d \leq 0.65$), indicates that female students tended to rate their expectations of becoming involved with their campus and outside communities higher than male students. Fifteen of the 28 showed a small effect size ($0.11 < d \leq 0.35$), while the remaining 12 subfactors had near-zero effect sizes. When individual Self-Efficacy items are considered at the subfactor level (shown in Table 3.3), one of 38 subfactors had a difference with a moderate effect size (3%), 21 of 38 had small effect sizes (55%), and the remaining 16 have near-zero effect sizes (42%). Overall, 97% of the subfactors had small to near-zero effect sizes (**Table 10**).

Exploratory Factor Analysis (EFA) was performed on the entire set of subfactors to determine if any subfactors formed natural groups which may indicate a pattern of consistently higher or lower effect sizes. Results of the EFA resulted in six natural groups; however, none of the indicated groups of subfactors showed a consistent propensity toward higher or lower effect sizes. Therefore, discussion of differences at the subfactor level will be based on individual subfactors rather than possible groupings of subfactors indicated through EFA.

Of the individual items in the assessment, two (1%) had effect sizes in the moderate range. Both items were within the Expectancy-Value construct. These questions were:

- As a freshman in college, I expect to pursue some sort of community service work outside of my regular course work, and

- I expect to make friends with students from my major and form a study group in order to improve my college learning experiences.

Of the remaining items, 76 (48%) had small effect sizes and 80 (51%) had near-zero effect sizes.

Small to near-zero effect sizes were found from 97% of the subfactors and 99% of the individual items when the data was taken in aggregate. Looking at the data from individual years (2004–2007) showed small to near-zero effect sizes from 92.1% - 100% of the subfactors and 94.3%– 99.4% of the individual items.

6.7 Cluster analysis

McDermott's three-stage cluster analysis was performed on the aggregate student population (2004–2007). The male population (n = 5644) was randomly sorted and divided into four groups; these four groups of male students and one group consisting of all female students (n = 1228) were analyzed and compared to determine similarity. Three clusters were indicated in each subset of students through the process, resulting in final solutions of three clusters for each group of male students and three clusters for female students.

Subfactor	**p** (MC)	**d**	
Exp-Value: *Community Involvement*	<.0001	−0.359	Moderate
Surface: *Studying**	<.0001	0.283	
Motivation: *Control**	<.0001	−0.277	
Major Decision: *Urgency**	<.0001	−0.261	
Deep: *Motive**	<.0001	−0.260	
Exp-Value: *Social Engagement**	<.0001	−0.241	
Exp-Value: *Academic Resources**	<.0001	−0.238	
Motivation: *Curiosity**	<.0001	−0.233	
Self-efficacy: *Study Skills**	<.0001	−0.206	
Leadership: *Motivation**	<.0001	−0.200	
Self-efficacy: *Writing Skills**	<.0001	−0.193	Small
Self-efficacy: *Physics**	<.0001	0.177	
Motivation: *Challenge**	<.0001	−0.165	
Major Decision: *Independence**	<.0001	0.159	
Self-efficacy: *Programming**	<.0001	0.158	
Leadership: *Self-Assessment**	0.0002	−0.149	
Major Decision: *Certainty of Decision**	<.0001	0.148	
Motivation: *Career**	<.0001	−0.146	
Self-efficacy: *Teaming Skills**	0.0001	−0.128	
Team vs. Individual: *Individual**	<.0001	0.124	
Self-efficacy: *Communication**	<.0001	−0.121	
Exp-Value: *Persistence**	<.0001	−0.119	
Self-efficacy: *Chemistry*	0.0345	−0.078	
Self-efficacy: *Problem Solving*	0.0248	−0.075	
Metanalysis: *Planning**	0.0089	0.065	
Team vs. Individual: *Team dynamic*	0.1237	−0.063	
Metanalysis: *Cognition*	0.0346	−0.062	
Self-efficacy: *Creative Thinking*	0.0587	−0.062	
Metanalysis: *Awareness*	0.0100	0.060	
Surface: *Memorization*	0.0475	−0.060	Near-zero
Self-efficacy: *Math*	0.0474	0.053	
Metanalysis: *Self-Checking*	0.1725	−0.052	
Leadership: *Planning*	0.2221	−0.052	
Deep: *Strategy*	0.0794	−0.046	
Leadership: *Teammates*	0.6053	0.035	
Major Decision: *Difficulty in Decisions*	0.4074	−0.013	
Major Decision: *Personal Issues*	0.6431	0.012	
Exp-Value: *Employment Opportunities*	0.8631	0.008	

Statistically significant difference, small to near-zero effect size.

Table 10.
Effect sizes at the subfactor level (including self-efficacy items).

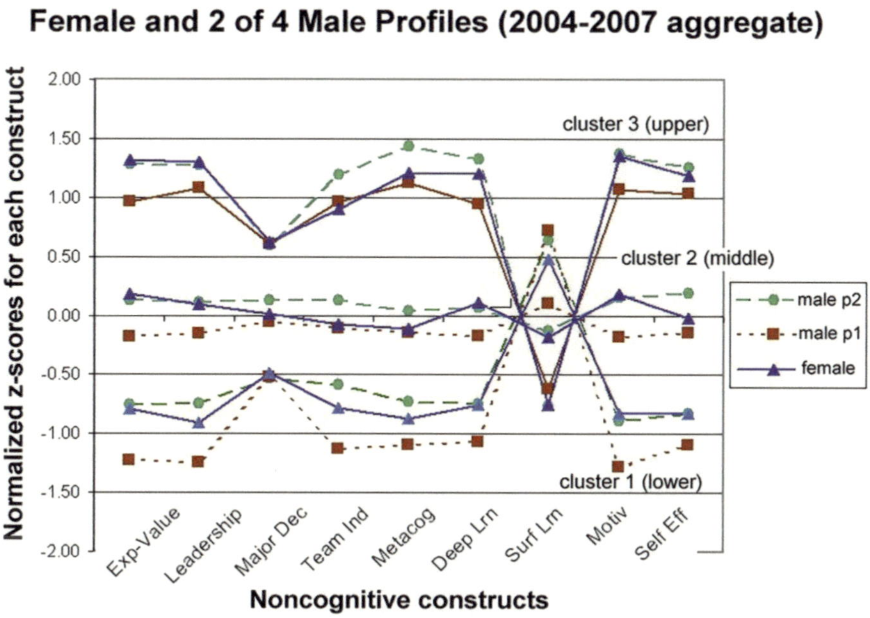

Figure 3.
Overlay plot showing three-cluster solutions for normative taxonomy: female students and two (of four) representative male student clusters.

Figure 3 shows an overlay of plots of the means of each construct for each cluster of male and female students. Constructs are on the x-axis, with center values (normalized z-scores) for each construct on the y-axis. Students in cluster 1 ("lower") responded approximately one standard deviation below the norm (with the exception of Surface Learning) while students in cluster 3 ("upper") responded one standard deviation above the average (with the exception of Surface Learning). Students in cluster 2 ("middle") clustered about the norms for each construct. Cluster numbers are used only to distinguish between groups - there is no significance to the cluster numbers.

Figure 3 shows that male profiles and female profiles have a consistent shape with minimal variation between sexes. Cattell's Cluster Similarity Coefficients were calculated to objectively determine the similarity between each cluster within and between sexes; values are shown in **Table 11**. Recall that excellent cluster similarity is demonstrated with values of Cattell's coefficient $r_p > 0.95$; values of Cattell's coefficient comparing each cluster with the corresponding cluster of the two sexes exceed 0.90, indicating good to excellent similarity. Absolute values of Cattell's coefficient comparing clusters between female students and any group of male students expected to be dissimilar were less than 0.7, indicating they were indeed dissimilar.

Coefficients of similarity, similar profiles in shape and pattern and similar percentages of students within each cluster demonstrate male and female student responses are indeed similar.

7. Discussion

The Student Attitudinal Success Instrument I, an instrument to assess nine affective/attitudinal characteristics (and their associated subscales) of incoming students

		Male 4			Male 3			Male 2			Female			Male 1		
		p3	**p2**	**p1**	**p3**	**p2**	**p1**	**p3**	**p2**	**p1**	**p3**	**p2**	**p1**	**p3**	**p2**	**p1**
Male 1	p1	−0.36	0.21		−0.29	0.40	**0.89**	−0.20	0.45	**0.93**	−0.23	0.39	**0.96**	−0.38	0.21	
	p2	0.39	**1.00**	0.23	0.54	**0.95**	−0.04	0.69	**0.93**	0.01	0.66	**0.94**	0.07	0.37		
	p3	**0.99**	0.37	−0.37	**0.96**	0.18	−0.49	**0.86**	0.13	−0.47	**0.90**	0.18	−0.44			
Female	p1	−0.43	0.06	**0.95**	−0.37	0.24	**0.96**	−0.30	0.29	**0.98**	−0.31	0.24				
	p2	0.20	**0.94**	0.41	0.33	**0.99**	0.11	0.49	**0.98**	0.17	0.46					
	p3	**0.91**	0.66	−0.22	**0.98**	0.46	−0.38	**0.99**	0.41	−0.35						
Male 2	p1	−0.46	0.01	**0.92**	−0.40	0.18	**0.99**	−0.33	0.22							
	p2	0.15	**0.92**	0.47	0.29	**1.00**	0.16	0.44								
	p3	**0.89**	0.70	−0.19	**0.96**	0.49	−0.36									
Male 3	p1	−0.49	−0.04	**0.88**	−0.43	0.12										
	p2	0.20	**0.95**	0.42	0.34											
	p3	**0.97**	0.54	−0.28												
Male 4	p1	−0.36	0.22													
	p2	0.40														
	p3															

Excellent similarity is indicated by $r_p > 0.95$ (expected similar cells are in bold), dissimilarity is indicated by $r_p < 0.70$.

Table 11.
Cattell's similarity coefficient values for 3 cluster solutions: female cluster and four male clusters, 2004–2007 aggregate population.

prior to the beginning of their program of study, was evaluated using data collected from large cohorts of incoming engineering students.

The SASI-I is shown to be a psychometrically sound instrument for the population of first-year engineering students at a large institution in the Midwest (United States). Internal consistency of scale scores was investigated. Factor analysis was used to establish and verify the structure of the factors and subfactors. Cronbach's coefficient alpha values for all scales exceed 0.8 (with two exceptions, 0.75 and 0.79); confirmatory factor analysis results verify the theoretical factor structure of each. McDermott's three-stage cluster analysis was used to define the normative taxonomies of 3 years of student data. Cluster analysis results in a stable, repeatable 3-cluster solution over multiple years: clusters expected to be highly similar were shown to have values of Cattell's coefficient > 0.94, providing evidence of stability.

This instrument is a tool to collect data prior to beginning classes in the first year of engineering, thus, it can provide valuable input to any model predicting retention past the first year (when most attrition in engineering occurs). In addition, this tool provides information on characteristics for which intervention methods may be developed, thus increasing likelihood of student success. Unlike other assessment instruments which rely on data collected during or after the first year or data for which a school may not have an influence, this tool provides necessary input for the creation and adoption of first-year programs at the earliest possible time.

Inputs to model(s) to be developed include these affective/attitudinal constructs in addition to cognitive data; such models will allow for guidance for individual students or small groups who may particularly benefit from specific intervention programs [51–54]. Cluster membership offers a potential model input that has previously not been presented in the literature within engineering. Additionally, students who may not experience a benefit from these interventions may be able to opt out of some first-year programs, thus increasing the value of the course/program content they will experience during their first year.

Finally, while this instrument is effective, additional affective/attitudinal characteristics which could prove to be predictive of retention have been incorporated into the SASI-2 [55]. Ideally, the size of the existing instrument could be reduced to allow for inclusion of additional constructs without increasing the number of items. Additional affective/attitudinal constructs to be investigated and eventually proposed for inclusion should include only those constructs for which first-year intervention programs can have an effect.

7.1 Support for the gender similarity hypothesis

The Gender Similarity Hypothesis theorizes that most psychological differences between male and female students are small ($0.11 < d \leq 0.35$) to near-zero ($d \leq 0.10$). Analysis of our noncognitive data certainly supports this hypothesis; although five of the nine superordinate constructs were found to have a statistically significant difference, the significance was due to the large sample size. Each construct was found to have an effect size that was small or near-zero. Furthermore, examination of the data from 2004 to 2007 showed each effect size for each construct was consistently low to near-zero.

Analysis of the data at the subfactor and individual item level also supports the hypothesis. At the subfactor level with data taken in aggregate, 97% of the subfactors and 99% of the individual items had small to near-zero effect sizes. Data from each year from 2004 to 2007 showed the lowest percentage of subfactors with small to near-zero effect sizes was 97% and the lowest percentage of individual items was 94%. This analysis certainly supports the Gender Similarity Hypothesis.

7.2 Normative taxonomies and the gender similarity hypothesis

A comparison between the sexes using cluster analysis certainly offers additional support for the Gender Similarity Hypothesis. Both male and female students tended to cluster into three very similar groups as evidenced visually (as seem in **Figure 3**) and as quantitatively measured by Cattell's similarity coefficient. Results from the cluster analysis show that the female and male populations were extremely similar, with similarity coefficients exceeding 0.90 between the female group and any group of male students.

Male and female students were remarkably similar in self-reported, affective characteristics prior to beginning their first year of study in engineering. Of particular interest are some characteristics dealing with student self-efficacy in math and science. There was not a statistically significant difference in student self-efficacy toward math ($p = 0.047$, $d = 0.053$) even given a large sample size. Data over the four-year period showed a small effect size in 2004 ($d = 0.124$) and near-zero in subsequent years ($d = 0.008$ in 2005, $d = -0.003$ in 2006 and $d = 0.07$ in 2007). While this is not sufficient evidence to prove any trend in a difference in self-efficacy in math, it is consistent with results as reported by Hyde.

Two areas in which effect sizes appear to be generally larger (although still small) are those dealing with community involvement (where females respond higher) and areas which deal with the control over the learning environment. Subscales within the Expectancy-Value construct including Community Involvement, Social Engagement and Academic Resources (dealing primarily with the expected use of group/community resources) appear toward the top of the list. Items in these subfactors deal with an individual and their involvement in a community. Community involvement does not correspond to involvement in a working group or team; for example, (Team vs. Individual) Team Dynamic and (Leadership) Teammates have near-zero effect sizes. These results tend to indicate that particular attention to the learning environment within engineering, particularly emphasizing involvement of the academic community is an important factor especially for female students.

Control over the individual learning environment subfactors include (Deep Learning) Motive, (Motivation) Control and (Major Decision) Urgency (to select a major). Items within these subfactors deal with the individual's determination of their personal learning goals. These results seem to indicate that female students may have a more personal interest in entering engineering. These results lead to a question requiring further study: studies show that female students tend to attribute failure to themselves as opposed to male students, who attribute failure to their environment. If female students enter engineering with a more personal interest, do male students surpass them in these characteristics over the first year, and if so, why?

8. Implications and further study

Results from this self-report instrument prior to the beginning of college indicate that there are few if any differences between female and male students in their self-reported affective characteristics. Other studies have suggested that female students tend to have a lower self-efficacy during or after their first year; if this is the case, there may be characteristics of the first year of engineering that have an effect on the confidence and self-efficacy of female students in particular.

Two theories that have been theorized as applicable to gender differences include the Expectancy Theory and the Cognitive Dissonance Theory.

The Expectancy Theory states that the motivation to succeed is the product of three factors: expectancy (the perceived effort/performance relationship), instrumentality (perceived performance/reward relationship) and valence (the value of the reward). It is possible that the emphasis on individual performance, the existence of perceived weed-out classes and lack of community common within many first-year engineering experiences may influence the expectancy and instrumentality of female students. Differences in measures dealing with community may influence expectancy; if an individual can better succeed as part of a community and they feel they are able to act only as an individual, they may tend to feel their performance is inadequate (expectancy). In turn they may feel their ability to obtain their goal is inadequate (instrumentality). Further work is necessary to validate the application of this theory.

The Cognitive Dissonance Theory relates multiple cognitions or beliefs: when two beliefs conflict, individuals will attempt to modify one or both to bring them into agreement. If the environment in the first year of engineering is one that emphasizes individual performance, competition and a lack of community, and if these characteristics are important to female students, they may gradually 'learn' that they should not be successful, which disagrees with their self-efficacy – their belief that they can be successful. Changing self-efficacy would reduce the conflict between these beliefs, which could lead to leaving engineering. As with the expectancy theory, studying the changes in self-report characteristics is needed to support this theory.

8.1 Limitations

While the data was from a series of large cohorts, all data was from a single institution in the Midwest region of the United States, so caution should be exercised if applying these results to other institutions or cohorts from different regions or countries. Further, this analysis applies to students who had applied and were admitted to engineering, and engineering admissions criteria almost certainly had an effect on the population of students whose affective characteristics were analyzed.

9. Conclusion

Student responses to an instrument to assess nine noncognitive characteristics (and their associated subfactors) prior to the beginning of their engineering program were used to study differences between male and female students. Overall, results strongly support the Gender Similarity Hypothesis, which theorizes that most differences between the sexes are small to near zero. Analysis of the data at the construct, subfactor and item level, as well as cluster analysis supported this hypothesis. In general, male and female students enter their first year of engineering with very similar affective characteristics.

There does seem to be evidence to support the idea that female students would be well served to emphasize activities associated with community, including both learning communities and community service. There also seems to be evidence to support investigating the environment of competition and individual achievement within first year programs. Female students seem to enter engineering with (slightly) more focus on achieving their goals, but there is evidence that female students have lower self-efficacy by the end of their first year. Identifying characteristics contributing to this change could lead to increased retention in engineering for students who enter college with a strong intent to succeed.

If female students and male students enter college with similar cognitive and non-cognitive characteristics, further investigation is needed to determine what characteristics of the first year of study lead to higher attrition among female students.

Majors with a history of predominantly male enrollment such as medicine and law have seen increasing numbers of female students in recent years. Despite efforts attempting to attract female students to engineering, the percentage of female students has remained relatively steady for the past few decades. If engineering is indeed a creative, innovative profession that deals with and helps society, the first year of study should reflect this as much as possible.

Acknowledgements

Many people contributed to this effort. The original work is based on a dissertation by the author, with exceptional contributions from Dr. P.K. Imbrie and Dr. Teri Reed (University of Oklahoma), Dr. Alice Pawley and Dr. David Radcliffe (Purdue University), and Dr. Joe J. J. Lin. Parts of this chapter were previously published in the doctoral thesis by the same author: Kenneth J. Reid, "Development of the Student Attitudinal Success Instrument: Assessment of First Year Engineering Students Including Differences by Gender," Purdue University, May 2009. Available from: URL: https://docs.lib.purdue.edu/dissertations/AAI3378850/.

Author details

Kenneth J. Reid
University of Indianapolis, Indianapolis, Indiana, United States

*Address all correspondence to: reidk@uindy.edu

References

[1] Reid K, Imbrie PK, Lin JJ, Reed T, Immekus J. Psychometric properties and stability of the student attitudinal success instrument: The SASI-I. International Journal of Engineering Education. 2016;**32**(6):2470-2486

[2] Bernold L, Spurlin J, Anson C. Understanding our students: A longitudinal study of success and failure in engineering with implications for increased retention. Journal of Engineering Education. 2007;**96**:263-274

[3] Bothaina A, Al-Sheeb A, Abdella G. Modeling of student academic achievement in engineering education using cognitive and non-cognitive factors. Journal of Applied Research in Higher Education. 2019;**11**(2):178-198

[4] Yoon S, Imbrie PK, Lin JJ, Reid K. Validation of the student attitudinal success inventory II for engineering students. In: Proceedings of the American Society for Engineering Education Annual Conference. Indianapolis, IN: American Society for Engineering Education; 2014

[5] Rosen J, Glennie E, Dalton B, Lennon J, Bozick R. Noncognitive Skills in the Classroom: New Perspectives on Educational Research. Research Triangle Park, NC: RTI International; 2010

[6] Imbrie P, Lin J, Reid K. Comparison of four methodologies for modeling student retention in engineering. In: Proceedings of the American Society for Engineering Education Annual Conference. Louisville, KY: American Society for Engineering Education; 2010

[7] Ting S. Predicting academic success of first-year engineering students from standardized test scores and psychosocial variables. International Journal of Engineering Education. 2001;**17**(1):75-80

[8] Besterfield-Sacre M, Atman C, Shuman L. Characteristics of freshman engineering students: Models for determining student attrition in engineering. Journal of Engineering Education. 1997;**86**(2):139-149

[9] Ohland M, Sheppard S, Lichtenstein G, Eris O, Chachra D, Layton R. Persistence, engagement, and migration in engineering programs. Journal of Engineering Education. 2008;**97**(3):259-278

[10] Al-Sheeb BA, Hamouda AM, Abdella GM. Modeling of student academic achievement in engineering education using cognitive and non-cognitive factors. Journal of Applied Research in Higher Education. 2019;**11**(2):178-198. DOI: 10.1108/JARHE-10-2017-0120

[11] Major JC, Scheidt M, Godwin A, Perkins H, Kim S, Self B, et al. Institutional characteristics and engineering student non-cognitive and affective (NCA) profiles. International Journal of Engineering Education. 2023, 2023;**39**(3):668-684

[12] Scheidt M, Godwin A, Berger E, Chen J, Self BP, Widmann JM, et al. Engineering students' noncognitive and affective factors: Group differences from cluster analysis. Journal of Engineering Education. 2021;**110**(2):343-370

[13] Virguez L, Murzi H, Reid K. A quantitative analysis of first-year engineering students' engineering-related motivational beliefs. International Journal of Engineering Education. 2021;**37**:6

[14] Besterfield-Sacre M, Moreno M, Shuman L, Atman C. Gender and ethnicity differences in freshman engineering student attitudes: A cross-institutional study. Journal of Engineering Education. 2021;**90**(4):477-490

[15] Reid K. Development of the student attitudinal success instrument: Assessment of first year engineering students including differences by gender [dissertation]. West Lafayette, IN: Purdue University; 2009

[16] French B, Oakes B. Measuring academic intrinsic motivation in the first year of college: Reliability and validity evidence for a new instrument. Journal of the First-Year Experience. 2003;**15**(1):83-102

[17] Bandura A. Perceived self-efficacy in cognitive development and functioning. Educational Psychologist. 1993;**28**(2):117-148

[18] Wigfield A, Eccles J. Expectancy–value theory of achievement motivation. Contemporary Educational Psychology. 2000;**25**:68-81

[19] Biggs J, Kember LD. The revised two-factor study process questionnaire: R-SPQ-2F. British Journal of Educational Psychology. 2001;**71**(1):133-149

[20] O'Neil H, Abedi J. Reliability and validity of a state metacognitive inventory: Potential for alternative assessment. The Journal of Educational Research. 1996;**89**(4):234-245

[21] Hayden D, Holloway E. A longitudinal study of attrition among engineering students. Engineering Education. 1985;**75**(7):664-668

[22] McMaster J. Desired attributes of an engineering graduate. In: Proceedings of the AIAA Advanced Measurement and Ground Testing Technology Conference. New Orleans, LA: American Institute of Aeronautics and Astronautics; 1996

[23] Osipow S. Assessing career indecision. Journal of Vocational Behavior. 1999;**55**(1):147-154

[24] Henson R. Understanding internal consistency reliability estimates: A conceptual primer on coefficient alpha. Measurement and Evaluation in Counseling and Development. 2001;**34**(3):177-189

[25] Nunnally J, Bernstein I. Psychometric Theory. 3rd ed. New York, NY: McGraw-Hill; 1994

[26] Alsawalmeh A, Feldt L. Testing the equality of two independent coefficients adjusted by the Spearman-Brown formula. Applied Psychological Measurement. 1999;**23**(4):363-370

[27] Bodnar G. Statistical analysis of multiple-choice exams. Journal of Chemical Education. 1980;**57**(3):188-190

[28] Hu L, Bentler P. Cutoff criteria for fit indexes in covariance structure analysis: Conventional criteria versus new alternatives. Structural Equation Modeling. 1999;**6**(1):1-55

[29] Tanguma J. Effects of sample size on the distribution of selected fit indices: A graphical approach. Educational and Psychological Measurements. 2001;**61**(5):759-776

[30] McDermott P. Megacluster analytic strategy for multistage hierarchical grouping with relocations and replications. Educational and Psychological Measurement. 1998;**58**:677-686

[31] Ward J. Hierarchical grouping to optimize an objective function. American Statistical Journal. 1993;**58**:236-244

[32] Duda R, Hart P. Pattern Classification and Scene Analysis. New York, NY: John Wiley; 1973

[33] Mojena R. Hierarchical grouping methods and stopping rules: An evaluation. The Computer Journal. 1977;**20**(4):359-363

[34] Tyron B, Bailey D. Cluster Analysis. New York, NY: McGraw Hill; 1970

[35] Cattell R. The Scientific Use of Factor Analysis in Behavioral and Life Sciences. New York, NY: Plenum Press; 1978

[36] Cohen J. Statistical Power Analysis for the Behavioral Sciences. 2nd ed. Hillsdale, NJ: Lawrence Earlbaum Associates; 1988

[37] Cohen J. A power primer. Psychological Bulletin. 1992;**112**(1):155-159

[38] Rosnow R, Rosenthal R. Computing contrasts, effect sizes, and counternulls on other people's published data: General procedures for research consumers. Psychological Methods. 1996;**1**(4):331-340

[39] Hyde J, Linn M. Gender similarities in mathematics and science. Science. 2006;**314**:599-600

[40] Hyde J. The gender similarity hypothesis. American Psychologist. 2005;**60**(6):581-592

[41] Streiner D. Starting at the beginning: An introduction to coefficient alpha and internal consistency. Journal of Personality Assessment. 2003;**80**(1):99-103

[42] Tuckman B. Conducting Educational Research. 5th ed. New York, NY: Wadsworth Group; 1999

[43] Alsawalmeh A, Feldt L. Testing the equality of two independent α coefficients adjusted by the Spearman-Brown formula. Applied Psychological Measurement. 1999;**23**(4):363-370

[44] Freedman R, Stumpf S. What can one learn from the learning style inventory? Academy of Management Journal. 1978;**21**(2):275-282

[45] Sanoff A. Competing forces. ASEE Prism. 2005;**15**(2):24-29

[46] National Academy of Engineering (NAE). Adapting Engineering Education to the New Century: Educating the Engineer of 2020. Washington D.C.: National Academies Press; 2005

[47] Hyde JS, Fennema E, Lamon SJ. Gender differences in math performance: A meta-analysis. Psychological Bulletin. 1990;**107**(2):139-155

[48] Hyde JS, Lindberg S, Linn M, Ellis A, Williams C. Gender similarities characterize math performance. Science. 2008;**321**:494-495

[49] National Assessment of Educational Progress (NAEP). Available from: http://nces.ed.gov/nationsreportcard/nde/ [Accessed 31 December 2024]

[50] Reid K, Imbrie PK. Noncognitive characteristics of incoming engineering students compared to incoming engineering technology students: A preliminary examination. In: Proceedings of the American Society for Engineering Education Annual Conference. Pittsburgh, PA: American Society for Engineering Education; 2008

[51] Imbrie PK, Lin JJ, Reid K. Comparison of four methodologies for modeling student retention in engineering. In: Proceedings of the American Society for Engineering Education Annual Conference. Louisville, KY: American Society for Engineering Education; 2010

[52] Imbrie PK, Lin JJ, Reid K, Malyscheff A. Using hybrid data to model student success in engineering with artificial neural networks. In: Proceedings of the Research in Engineering Education Symposium. Davos, Switzerland: Research in Engineering Education Network; 2008

[53] Imbrie PK, Lin JJ, Oladunni T, Reid K. Use of a neural network model and noncognitive measures to predict student matriculation in engineering. In: Proceedings of the American Society for Engineering Education Annual Conference. Honolulu, HI: American Society for Engineering Education; 2007

[54] Geisinger B, Raj RD. Why they leave: Understanding student attrition from engineering majors. International Journal of Engineering Education. 2013;**29**(4):914-925

[55] Yoon S, Imbrie PK, Lin JJ, Reid K. Validation of the student attitudinal success inventory II for engineering students. In: Proceedings of the American Society for Engineering Education Annual Conference. Indianapolis, IN: American Society for Engineering Education; 2014

Chapter 7

Computerized Child Attention Test

Mirta Susana Ison

Abstract

The Child Attention Test 6.0 (TAI) was developed to assess attentional performance and visuospatial working memory in children from 8 to 11 years old through visual search tasks that involve putting into practice the perception of differences, visual discrimination, visual integration, perceptual speed, and memory of visuospatial information. It is an instrument that has validity and reliability indicators. It can be used in both clinical and educational settings. It has the advantage of having parallel forms to be applied in the case of studies with experimental research designs, such as before and after any intervention, or for monitoring of clinical or educational training programs.

Keywords: computerized attention test, evaluation, training, sustained attention, visual working memory

1. Introduction

The Child Attention Test 6.0 ("TAI") was carried out by Ison & Arroyo [1], based on previous versions of the test [2, 3]. It has been developed to assess attentional performance and visuospatial working memory in children aged 8 to 11 years through visual search tasks involving putting into practice the perception of differences, visual discrimination, visual integration, perceptual speed, and memory of visuospatial information. As we know, attention and working memory are basic cognitive processes developed gradually during childhood and fundamental for school learning [4–7].

Attention has been defined as a multidimensional construct responsible for regulating which stimuli perceptual resources are directed toward, filtering irrelevant information in order to promote the retention of information for a period before acting on it [8–10]. Attention is a good indicator for predicting the degree of performance in tasks involving executive control. Studies carried out in both children and adults have highlighted that this is important for greater attentional capacity and better performance in cognitive tasks [11–13].

In its part, working memory (WM) is defined as a store of limited capacity storing information for a short period of time. In other words, it maintains and manipulates this information temporarily but also processes and uses this information in an active way depending on the objectives and tasks that the subject must solve [9, 14, 15].

IntechOpen

Further, it involves keeping the information in mind and manipulating it in some way to understand and acquire more complex knowledge, using and integrating that information into a coherent whole [16]. Thus, a close link has been recognized between attention, perception, and the basic components of executive functioning: inhibitory control, working memory, and cognitive flexibility [13, 17–19].

Various studies have shown the bidirectionality between the development of attention systems and working memory performance in early childhood [8–10, 20, 21]. These bidirectional effects are common and noted across development, and, therefore, the potential influence of working memory on the later development of attention systems in infancy and early childhood is equally interesting.

The assessment of attention in children has mainly been concentrated on the paradigm of visuospatial search, which requires the capacity for visual discrimination, precision, and perceptual speed, maintaining the focus of attention to ignore distracting stimuli or inhibit incompatible responses. However, as Lezak et al. [22] argue, it is difficult to find a test that measures only one cognitive construct, and this aspect is clearly reflected in attention tests. The tests used to evaluate attention could also take into account visual-motor coordination, perceptual inhibition, visual working memory, speed of processing, and mental flexibility. The usual tests to evaluate attention are the d2 Attention Test, WAIS-IV Cues and Symbol Search, Trail Making Test, Continuous Performance Task, and CARAS-R Difference Perception Test, among others.

The conceptual foundation of the TAI test considers attention as a multidimensional construct interrelated with basic processes of inhibitory control, working memory, and cognitive flexibility. These are central components of executive functioning [8, 9, 13].

The computerized evaluation of attention and working memory has been gaining relevance both in research and in professional practice. Thus, it is of interest to achieve the greatest possible precision in the evaluation of these functions [23], as well as to promote their development through systematic practice with the implementation of programs for their stimulation and strengthening.

The Computerized Child Attention Test (TAI 6.0) brings together these two large modules in the same software: the evaluation module on the one hand and the training module through a routine to strengthen functions on the other hand. This instrument can be used in both clinical and educational settings, allowing the early detection of difficulties in the evaluated functions.

Firstly, in the evaluation module, all participants are assessed in the same way by means of a standard presentation of stimuli in terms of their organization and complexity. The aim is to assess attentional control through tasks that require locating key stimuli among a wider set of stimuli that act as distractors, deploying a series of perceptual-attentional and mnemonic skills. In the interpretation of the performances obtained, both in attention and in visuospatial working memory, the time variable is incorporated.

Secondly, the *training module* presents various recreational activities, with increasing levels of difficulty aimed at exercising focus, attentional maintenance, and visuospatial working memory, all through visual search tasks.

TAI in version 6.0 was developed using Unity 2018, which allows creating games and applications for various platforms, such as Windows, Linux, Mac, Android, and iOS, among others. This development engine was selected for its ease of use for 2D games, its compatibility with Android, and its ability to export data in other formats. This multipurpose video game development engine allows working in both 2D and 3D.

However, this version 6.0 only used 2D, the main tool with which both the evaluation and training modules were developed.

The software collects and stores the results obtained in a database, allowing an in-depth analysis of the performance obtained by the participants. The results can be exported in a format readable by Excel and then used by any data processing software, among which one of the most used is Statistical Package for Social Sciences (SPSS).

Since the first version made by Ison et al. [2] until the current one, a series of modifications and updates were made due to advances in the development of software and information registration systems. These computerized recording systems are especially relevant for the evaluation and interpretation of psychological functions.

In this new version, TAI 6.0, analysis and color adjustment of the different stimuli were carried out, both in the evaluation and training modules, to prevent children with some type of undetected color blindness from failing to correctly perform the various activities due to their condition.

2. Brief description of the TAI 6.0 evaluation and training modules

All stimuli and scenarios used in both the evaluation and training modules were designed exclusively for the development of this software. The activities corresponding to each of them are based on tasks that involve an effort in attentional control in which the child must locate the significant stimuli among a broader set of stimuli acting as distractors, deploying a series of perceptual-attentional and mnemonic skills. The visual search tasks used in TAI 6.0 consist of visual discrimination activities through the perception of differences and similarities, visuospatial integration, perceptual speed, visual-motor coordination, and visuospatial recognition memory.

2.1 Evaluation module

This is intended for the evaluation of focused, sustained attention and visual working memory. It is characterized by having a standard presentation of stimuli so that all participants can be evaluated in the same way in terms of the organization and complexity of the task. It presents two parallel forms to be used in the case of studies with experimental research designs and can be applied both before and after any type of intervention or applied to monitor clinical training programs [24].

To select whether it is used to evaluate attention or visual working memory, a configuration panel opens, through which the function to be evaluated can be selected. The first two subtests evaluate focused and sustained attention, while the third test evaluates visual working memory. They are briefly described below:

2.1.1 Subtest "Looking for identical drawings"

The functions evaluated are focused attention and sustained visual attention. It has the advantage of measuring the reaction time for each stimulus. As seen in **Figures 1** and **2**, on the left side of the screen, the key model is presented, and, on the right side, stimuli that are the same, similar, or different to the model appear randomly.

Prior to the beginning of this evaluation subtest, this activity is practiced through a rehearsal session so that the child understands the meaning of the task that must be

Figure 1.
Examples of stimuli used in subtest 1 of TAI 6.0.

Figure 2.
Examples of stimuli used in subtest 1 of TAI 6.0 —parallel form. Note: Since the test is administered in Spanish, terms in that language are included in **Figures 1** *and 2. If the stimulus that appears in the right window is the same as the model on the left, the child clicks on* "Si" *(Yes in English), and a sound is heard immediately, as long as the choice is correct, with the words* "Muy bien" *(Very good in English) appearing and said by the character of a bird, and a new figure emerges. If this new figure is different from the model, the child must click* "No" *(No in English), and a new figure appears. If, however, the child makes a mistake by choosing an incorrect figure, a different sound indicating the error is heard, and the bird character says* "Presta atención" *(pay attention in English).*

performed. Subsequently, the subtest is administered to evaluate focused and sustained visual attention. The subtest is carried out with one of the 2 preset key stimuli, and the presentation of stimuli that appear has a pre-assigned order. The key prefixed stimuli are the dog and the car.

The time used to perform this subtest is expressed in seconds. It consists of a total of 90 stimuli. The software records the number of correct answers, errors of commission, and errors of omission in two times: partial time, previously scheduled at 180 seconds; and total time, corresponding to the entire time in which the child finished the subtest.

Four measures of attentional performance are obtained. The first of them is the partial direct score (PDS), in which the net successes are recorded up to 180 seconds from the start of the activity; that is, the successes (S) are counted, from which the sum of errors of commission (Ec) and errors of omission (Eo) are subtracted [25]. The second measure is the direct score in total time (DST), for which the same formula was applied, with only the number of total S, Ec, and Eo that the child executed at the end of the 90 stimuli counted. The third measure analyzes attentional effectivenwess in total time (AET), evaluating the joint use of attentional selectivity and maintenance skills, providing a measure of the accuracy with which a child manages to discriminate the 'key stimulus' within a set of similar stimuli [26]. Finally, in the fourth measure, attentional efficiency is analyzed in total time (AFT), which provides a measure of the child's ability to regulate, optimize, and maintain the attentional mechanism for a prolonged period. For this fourth measure, the time factor is incorporated in order to know the time interval that each child requires [24, 27].

2.1.2 Subtest "the farm"

The functions evaluated in this subtest are visual perceptual discrimination, sustained visual attention, visuospatial skills, and perceptual speed. The exercise consists of the search for similarities, discriminating differences within a wide and varied stimulating field (**Figure 3**). It also has a parallel form (**Figure 4**). As in the previous subtest, it begins with a practice so that the child understands the task that must be performed. Then, the evaluation subtest is administered with one of the 2 preset key stimuli, which, in this subtest, are the hen and, for the parallel form, the chick. The presentation of the same, different, or similar stimuli to the key stimulus is all shown on the screen and has a pre-assigned order.

This subtest consists of the presentation of 40 stimuli distributed on the screen, of which 15 are the correct stimuli that the child must select to respond correctly to

Figure 3.
Examples of stimuli belonging to subtest 2 of TAI 6.0.

Figure 4.
Examples of stimuli belonging to subtest 2 of TAI 6.0—parallel form. Note: Since the test is administered in Spanish, terms in that language are included in **Figures 3** *and* **4**. *On the right side, the key model indicated with the sign "Buscado" (wanted in English) is presented, and, on the screen, a farm is presented with 'chickens' stimuli that are the same, similar, or different to the model. The task is to look for stimuli equal to the model. If the indicated option is correct, a green check mark appears, showing the phrase "Muy bien" (very good in English), said by the bird character along with a characteristic sound. On the contrary, if the indicated option is incorrect, a red cross and the phrase "Presta atención" (pay attention in English) appear, followed by a sound different from the previous one but characteristic of incorrect answers.*

the instruction. The maximum score, 15, is a constant for the participants since the subtest does not end without first having found all the same stimuli. Three measurements are obtained. First is the direct score in total time (DST), obtained by recording the correct answers (S) and subtracting the errors (E) [25]. The second measure is attentional effectiveness in total time (AET) [27], and the third, attentional efficiency in total time (AFT) [27], both previously described.

2.1.3 Subtest "Looking for partners"

The function evaluated by this subtest is visual working memory. The proposed activities follow the logic of the memotest (**Figure 5**).

In the evaluation module, eight pairs of stimuli are displayed and distributed on the screen. Each pair is made up of the same stimuli, but the pairs of stimuli are not repeated, meaning that the 8 pairs of stimuli are different from each other. When the test starts, all the stimuli that make up the 8 pairs are shown. The screen duration of each stimulus is 2 seconds for each pair. Thus, the 8 pairs remain in the child's view for 16 seconds (**Figure 5A**). After this time has elapsed, the stimuli are hidden behind blue bubbles, and the test begins counting the time (**Figure 5B**). Every time the child clicks on a bubble, it reveals its contents. When a second bubble is clicked, it also shows its contents, indicating whether they are the same or different. If they are the same, the pair is visible, with the words "Very good" appearing, as said by the bird character (**Figure 5C**). If they are different, another sound indicating an error is heard, the 'bird character' says "Pay attention," and both stimuli are then hidden again (**Figure 5D**). The activity ends when all the pairs are found and the total time is recorded.

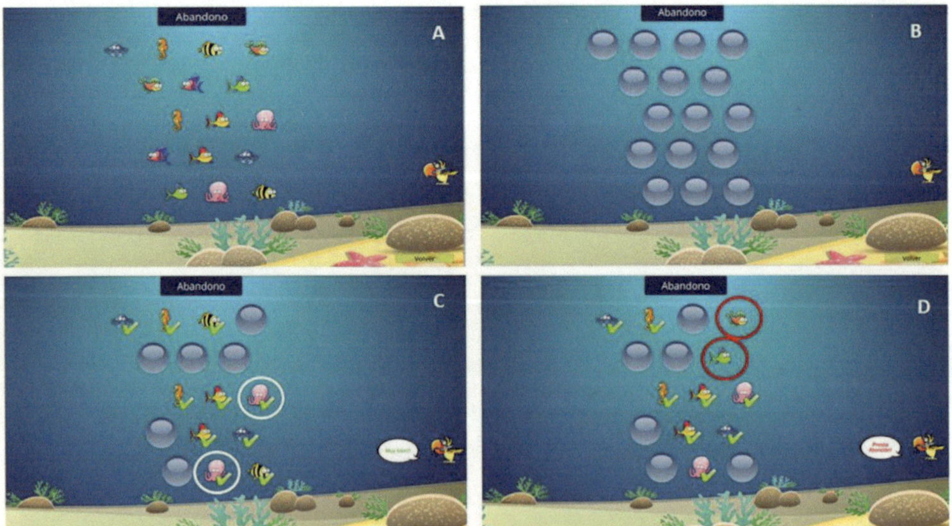

Figure 5.
Examples of stimuli used in subtest 3 of TAI 6.0. Note: Since the test is administered in Spanish, terms in that language are included in **Figure 5***. For 16 seconds, a screen with animals in the sea is presented. The task is to remember the location of each one of them. The task is to find the same pairs. If the pair of stimuli is found, the bird character utters the words* "Muy bien" *(very good in English). Otherwise, it says* "Presta atención" *(pay attention in English).*

Taking into account that the evaluation does not have a time limit and that the activity ends when the child manages to find all the same pairs, the found pairs (FP) value is a constant that always gives a total of 8 points, which is the total number of pairs found. That is why the variability of performance among children is given by the number of pairs not found (PNF) or errors. Based on this, the direct score in total time (DST) is achieved by subtracting the not-found pairs from the found pairs.

In turn, based on previous work [26–28], a formula was implemented to obtain working memory effectiveness (WME), which is equal to the sum of the pairs found divided by the number of attempts. The number of attempts implies the total FP plus PNF. A final measure is working memory efficiency (WMF), developed based on the study by Monteoliva et al. [27], and, for this, the time factor used to complete the test is taken into account. Thus, efficiency in visual working memory is obtained by dividing the pairs found by the total time spent performing this test [24]. Finally, regarding the results of this subtest, the software offers two options. On the one hand, a screen can be viewed detailing the performance of the evaluation. It shows the reaction times expressed in milliseconds that the child used in each of the answers, the number of successes and errors made, and, on the other hand, a graph that summarizes the general performance through the cognitive performance formulas for each test activity.

2.2 Training module

This module is intended to exercise focusing, attentional maintenance, and visuospatial working memory through visual search tasks across different recreational activities. In the training sessions, the expert explains the task that must be performed to the child and, at the same time, shows the child the characteristics of each exercise on the computer screen. Then, the child practices for a few minutes until it is confirmed that the task was perfectly understood. During the training, the expert could guide and help the child by explaining what is necessary in order to promote the implementation of metacognitive strategies in the student to carry out each recreational activity. Self-monitoring and self-regulation are thus encouraged in order to strengthen the cognitive functions to be trained.

In this module, there are 3 levels of complexity: easy, medium, and difficult. The complexity of the stimuli refers to how different the stimuli are that appear randomly with the key model. In turn, the expert is able to vary the level of complexity of the stimuli to exercise the different psychological functions, according to the characteristics and possibilities of the child. If considered necessary, the expert can enter a time limit for carrying out the activities. After that time, the activity is automatically cut off. If, however, no time limit is set, the program counts the total time spent by the child to carry out the training activity.

The activities of the training module follow the logic of those proposed in the evaluation module, but different stimuli are used in order of increasing complexity.

Three types of training activities are proposed.

2.2.1 Activity

This is composed of a series of games aimed at strengthening focused and sustained attention through the search for identical drawings. On the left side of the screen, the key model is presented, and, on the right side, stimuli, which are the same, similar, or different to the model, appear randomly. If the stimulus that appears in the right window is the same as the model, the child clicks "YES," and a sound is then heard immediately whenever the choice is correct, with the word "Very good" appearing from the character of a bird, and a new figure appears. If that new figure is different from the model, the child must click "NO," and a new figure appears. If, however, the child makes a mistake by choosing an incorrect figure, a different error sound appears, and the "bird character" says, "Pay more attention." The images shown in **Figure 6** are presented for illustrative purposes.

2.2.2 Activity 2

The functions to strengthen are visual perceptual discrimination, sustained visual attention, visuospatial skills, and perceptual speed. The exercise consists of the search for similarities and the discrimination of differences within a wide and varied stimulating field. In activity 2, two versions are presented for the training of attentional functions, the Farm (A) and the City (B), both variants with 8 different stimuli each and with different levels of complexity and quantity of stimuli (**Figure 7**).

It should be noted that the stimuli located in the middle zone are those pre-set and are the ones used for the evaluation module. Therefore, in the training module, both stimuli remain blocked. This happens for both activities: The Farm and the City. In **Figure 7**, they are marked with a yellow circle. In both the Farm and the City activities, on the right side, the key model indicated with the "Wanted" sign is presented, and the expert can select the number of stimuli that appear on the screen and the level of complexity of the activity. In both the Farm and the City activities, on the right side, the key model indicated with the "Wanted" sign is presented, and the expert can select the number of stimuli that appear on the screen, as well as the level of complexity of the activity. The task is to look for stimuli equal to the model. If the indicated option is correct, a green check mark appears, with the phrase "Very good" said by the bird character, along with a characteristic sound. On the contrary, if the indicated option is incorrect, a red cross and the phrase "Pay attention" appear, followed by a different sound characteristic of incorrect answers.

2.2.3 Activity 3

The functions to strengthen visuospatial work memory. The screen shows animals in the sea. This task uses memotest logic. The task is to remember the location of each of the sea animals in each drawing. The images are presented on the screen for 30 seconds and then turned around. The task is to find the same pairs. If the pair of

Figure 6.
Example of Activity 1 to stimulate focused and sustained attention in the search for identical drawings. Note: Since the test is administered in Spanish, terms in that language are included in **Figure 6**. "Muy Bien" *(very good in English) or* "Presta atención" *(pay attention in English) is said by the bird.* "Abondono" *(cancel in English),* "si" *(yes in English), and* "no" *(no in English) are also terms shown on the screen.*

Figure 7.
Example of Activity 2-A and 2-B to stimulate visual perceptual discrimination, visual sustained attention, visuospatial skills, and perceptual speed. Note: Similar Spanish terms are used as in **Figure 6**, *with the other terms in self-explanatory context.*

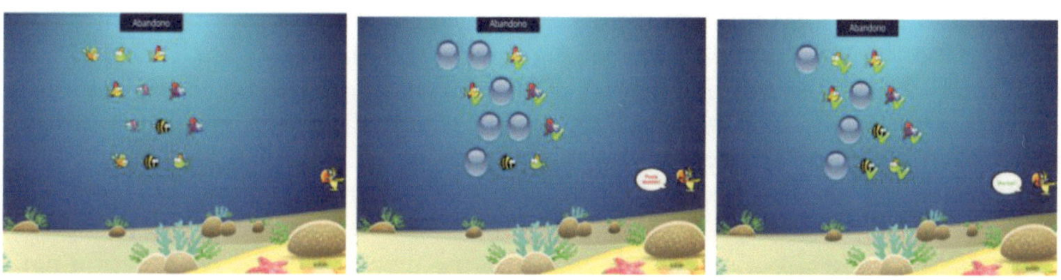

Figure 8.
Example of Activity 3 to stimulate visuospatial working memory. Note: "Abandono" *means canceled in English.*

stimuli is found, the bird character utters the word "Very good." Otherwise, it says, "Pay attention" (**Figure 8**).

The training module also has a results panel in which the performance obtained by the children in each activity carried out is displayed. Two performance measures are obtained. First is Attentional Effectiveness in order to analyze the accuracy in discriminating the "key stimulus" within a set of similar stimuli [26]. The second refers to Attentional Efficiency, which provides a measure of the child's ability to regulate, optimize, and maintain the attentional mechanism for a prolonged period.

3. Discussion

Attention and working memory are fundamental executive processes for learning and school performance, which both develop gradually during childhood.

Attention plays a key role in children's cognitive development, as it is responsible for regulating which stimuli perceptual resources will be directed to, filtering irrelevant information in order to promote the retention and recovery of information in working memory [8, 9, 12, 19]. It has a significant impact on school performance in a variety of tasks that take advantage of visuospatial working memory [7, 9] and interference control by avoiding internal or external distracting stimuli and shifting the attentional focus from one aspect of the stimulus to another when the situation requires it [6, 12].

Thus, the core of executive functioning is made up of highly interrelated and interdependent processes sharing a common denominator as an underlying factor of executive attention. Its adequate performance and strengthening are essential for the functioning of three central executive functions, such as inhibitory control, working memory, and cognitive flexibility, components that represent significant aspects in the regulation of information processing [12, 19–21].

Childhood is an optimal period for developing these functions, which can be strengthened with practice through the implementation of stimulation and strengthening programs.

In the province of Mendoza, Argentina, the author of this chapter has been a pioneer in the design and development of this computerized test [2, 3]. Thus, TAI has been used in various investigations in the school population [2, 3, 29–31].

The TAI presents satisfactory values of internal consistency for each of the tests (Test 1, KR20 = .78; Test 2, KR20 = .74; Test 3, KR20 = .73). Regarding concurrent validity, the results showed moderate and significant positive correlations ($p < .01$) between the CARAS-R test and subtests 1 and 2 of the TAI, used to evaluate attentional efficiency. Likewise, positive and significant associations ($p < .01$) were observed between Test 3 of the TAI and the Corsi Block Test, used to evaluate visuospatial working memory. These findings suggest that the TAI presents proper indicators of validity and reliability.

In Argentina, studies have been carried out that are strongly supported from an empirical and theoretical point of view on the validation of computerized instruments that evaluate attention and the central components of executive functioning: inhibitory control, working memory, and cognitive flexibility [18, 32–34].

The computerized battery called Cognitive Self-Regulation Tasks (TAC) was developed in Argentina for the computerized evaluation of executive functions in adults and children [33]. In a sample of 41 children between 6 and 11 years old, the internal consistency obtained through Cronbach's alpha was .79.

A widely used computerized test battery is the Cambridge Neuropsychological Test Automated Battery (CANTAB). It assesses visual memory, basic executive functions, and attention. It has acceptable internal consistency obtained from a sample of 230 children from Finland [35]. Cronbach's alpha values for the various subtests ranged from .49 to .87.

The Computerized Neuropsychological Assessment Battery for Children (BENCI), a test from Spain, was designed to assess various neuropsychological functions in Spanish-speaking children. It covers the assessment of attention, memory, processing speed, visual-motor coordination, language, and executive functions, but it has not yet been validated for the Argentine population [36].

The development of computerized programs for the evaluation and training of cognitive functions, based on empirical research, is extremely necessary for their incorporation and application, both in the processes of psychological diagnoses and for planning interventions in the clinical and educational areas.

Likewise, the administration of computerized tests allows for increasing the precision in the recording of the times used by the subjects to complete the test, reducing errors in the qualification of the results, and accelerating the process of obtaining the results. Equally important is the storage and safeguarding of the information of each person evaluated, reducing the time elapsed between the application of the evaluation and/or intervention instrument and the reporting of the results, among other considerations [23, 37].

In agreement with Canet Juric et al. [32], who have proposed that, for Spanish-speaking Latin American children, computerized tools for the evaluation of these functions have been scarce and not adequately validated or standardized for our country. From this perspective, TAI is a test developed and validated in our country that can be applied in clinical and educational settings, allowing us to reach more appropriate conclusions, both at the diagnostic level and in the interpretation of the results of neuropsychological interventions. Furthermore, it can be applied both to healthy populations and to populations with some neuropsychological dysfunction or difficulty. I am of the understanding that there are no similar tests in Latin America.

For future advances, it would be interesting if TAI could be applied in diverse contexts with other child populations in order to enable the identification of similarities and differences in the performance of the functions analyzed in different sociocultural groups, enriching the purpose of the test with comparative studies.

4. Conclusion

This chapter presents the development of the Computerized Child Attention Test, version 6.0 (TAI), an instrument made to assess attentional performance and visuospatial working memory in Argentine children from 8 to 11 years old through visual search tasks. This involves putting into practice the perception of differences, visual discrimination, visual integration, perceptual speed, and the memory of visuospatial information.

One of the advantages of TAI 6.0 is having parallel forms to be applied in the case of studies, where it is necessary: to evaluate the trajectory of attentional processes and visual working memory; to investigate the effectiveness of clinical or educational training programs; and to analyze the performances before and after the evaluated functions. In turn, the evaluation module has reliability and validity studies that make it an appropriate instrument for Argentine children, allowing the early detection of difficulties in the functions evaluated [24].

TAI meets the aforementioned conditions, being a complete tool, including, within the same software, both the Evaluation Module and the Training Module assessing attention and visuospatial working memory.

In relation to the training module, the software allows for obtaining a precise record of the trajectories of both functions as the training sessions progress, obtaining a performance profile. At the same time, reaction times, successes, errors, and omissions are recorded in each work session, while the results obtained by each child are safeguarded.

The contribution made with the development of TAI 6.0 is by offering a computerized instrument for application in child psychology, making it possible, in an integrated manner, to evaluate and strengthen two basic cognitive functions for school learning: attention and visuospatial working memory.

Acknowledgements

This work has been written within the framework of the two research projects. The first, 129/23 C.S., supported by the University of Aconcagua, and the second, PIP 2017-2019, N° 11220170100664, supported by the National Council for Scientific and Technical Research (CONICET- Argentina).

The author gratefully acknowledges David Beach for the English edition.

Conflict of interest

The author declares no conflict of interest.

Author details

Mirta Susana Ison
Psychology College, Aconcagua University and Human, Social and Environmental Science Institute (INCIHUSA) - National Scientific and Technical Research Council (CONICET), Mendoza, Argentina

*Address all correspondence to: mison@uda.edu.ar; mison@mendoza-conicet.gob.ar

References

[1] Ison M, Arroyo MJ. Test de Atención Infantil [software]. Versión 6.0. Buenos Aires: CONICET; 2023

[2] Ison MS, Soria ER, Ana D. Child Attention Test. Buenos Aires: CONICET; 2003

[3] Ison MS. Attentional capacity in children: Intervention programs for its development. In: Gargiullo PA, Mesones-Arroyo HL, editors. Psychiatry and Neuroscience Update. Switzerland: Springer; 2015. pp. 243-252. DOI: 10.1007/978-3-319-17103-6

[4] Clearfield MW. Play for success: A novel intervention to boost visual attention in low-socioeconomic-status infants. Journal of Experimental Child Psychology. 2020;**191**:104810. DOI: 10.1016/j.jecp.2020.104810

[5] Ison MS, González DF, Korzeniowski C. Strengthening socio-cognitive and emotional skills in early education through a school-based program: Preliminary study. European Journal of Psychology and Educational Research. 2020;**3**(2):87-100. DOI: 10.12973/ejper.3.2.87

[6] Korpa T, Skaloumbakas C, Katsounas M, Papadopoulou P, Lytra F, Karagianni S, et al. EF train: Development of an executive function training program for preschool and school-aged children with ADHD. International Journal of Psychology & Psychological Therapy. 2020;**20**(1):13-27

[7] Mathy F, Friedman O. Working memory develops at a similar rate across diverse stimuli. Journal of Experimental Child Psychology. 2020;**191**:104735. DOI: 10.1016/j.jecp.2019.104735

[8] Amso D, Scerif G. The attentive brain: Insights from developmental cognitive neuroscience. Nature Reviews Neuroscience. 2015;**16**(10):606-619. DOI: 10.1038/nrn4025

[9] Reynolds GD, Romano AC. The development of attention systems and working memory in infancy. Frontiers in Systems Neuroscience. 2016;**10**:15. DOI: 10.3389/fnsys.2016.00015

[10] Slattery EJ, Ryan P, Fortune DG, McAvinue LP. Contributions of working memory and sustained attention to children's reading achievement: A commonality analysis approach. Cognitive Development. 2021;**58**:101028. DOI: 10.1016/j.cogdev.2021.101028

[11] Boen R, Ferschmann L, Vijayakumar N, Overbye K, Fjell AM, Espeseth T, et al. Development of attention networks from childhood to young adulthood: A study of performance, intraindividual variability and cortical thickness. Cortex. 2021;**138**:138-151. DOI: 10.1016/j.cortex.2021.01.018

[12] Reindl E, Völter CJ, Campbell-May J, Call J, Seed AM. Exploring the development of attentional set shifting in young children with a novel intradimensional/extradimensional shift task. Journal of Experimental Child Psychology. 2022;**221**:105428. DOI: 10.1016/j.jecp.2022.105428

[13] Zelazo PD, Blair CB, Willoughby MT. Executive Function: Implications for Education (NCER 2017-2000). Washington, DC: National Center for Education Research; 2016. Available from: http://ies.ed.gov/

[14] Baddeley A. Working memory. Science. 1992;**255**(5044):556-559. DOI: 10.1126/science.1736359

[15] Passarotti AM, Balaban L, Colman LD, Katz LA, Trivedi N, Liu L, et al. A preliminary study on the functional benefits of computerized working memory training in children with pediatric bipolar disorder and attention deficit hyperactivity disorder. Frontiers in Psychology. 2020;**10**:3060. DOI: 10.3389/fpsyg.2019.03060

[16] Ison MS, Espósito A. Strategies for Cognitive and Socio-Emotional Development in Initial Education. Argentina: Aconcagua University; 2024. Manuscript submitted for publication

[17] Ariës RJ, Ghysels J, Groot W, Maassen van den Brink H. Combined working memory capacity and reasoning strategy training improves reasoning skills in secondary social studies education: Evidence from an experimental study. Thinking Skills and Creativity. 2016;**22**:233-246. DOI: 10.1016/j.tsc.2016.10.008

[18] Canet Juric L, Vernucci S, Zamora E, Introzzi I, Andrés ML. Analysis of omission and commission errors in a visual search task by school-age children. Studies in Psychology. 2021;**42**(1):47-75

[19] Diamond A. Executive functions. In: Handbook of Clinical Neurology. Vol. 173. Netherlands: Elsevier; 2020. pp. 225-240. DOI: 10.1016/B978-0-444-64150-2.00020-4

[20] Posner MI, Rothbart MK. Attention to learning of school subjects. Trends in Neuroscience and Education. 2014;**3**(1):14-17. DOI: 10.1016/j.tine.2014.02.003

[21] Astle DE, Scerif G. Interactions between attention and visual short-term memory (VSTM): What can be learnt from individual and developmental differences? Neuropsychologia. 2011;**49**:1435-1445. DOI: 10.1016/j.neuropsychologia.2010.12.001

[22] Lezak MD, Howieson DB, Bigler ED, Tranel D. Neuropsychological Assessment. 5th ed. New York: Oxford University Press; 2012. 1161 p

[23] Burga LA. Aplicaciones de la tecnología a la evaluación psicométrica. Propósitos y Representaciones. 2019;**7**(SPE):e318. DOI: 10.20511/pyr2019.v7nSPE.318

[24] Ison MS, Arroyo MJ, Caligiore-Gei MG. Test de Atención Infantil: análisis de las características psicométricas y valores de referencia preliminares. Avances en Psicología Latinoamericana. 2023;**41**(3):1-20. DOI: 10.12804/revistas.urosario.edu.co/apl/a.11903

[25] Ison MS, Anta FG. Estudio normativo del Test de Percepción de Diferencias (CARAS) en niños mendocinos. Interdisciplinaria. 2006;**23**(2):203-232

[26] Ison MS, Carrada MA. Evaluación de la eficacia atencional: estudio normativo preliminar en escolares argentinos. Revista Iberoamericana de Diagnóstico y Evaluación Psicológica (RIDEP). 2011;**29**(1):129-146. Available from: https://www.redalyc.org/pdf/4596/459645441008.pdf

[27] Monteoliva JM, Ison MS, Pattini AE. Evaluación del desempeño atencional en niños: eficacia, eficiencia y rendimiento. Interdisciplinaria. 2014;**31**(2):213-225. DOI: 10.16888/interd.2014.31.2.2

[28] Monteoliva JM, Carrada M, Ison MS. Test de Percepción de Diferencias: estudio normativo del desempeño atencional en escolares argentinos. Interdisciplinaria. 2017;**34**(1):39-56. DOI: 10.16888/interd.2017.34.1.3

[29] Ison MS. Intervention program to improve attention skills in argentine schoolchildren. International Journal of Psychological Research. 2011;**4**(2):72-79

[30] Menechelli EM, Espósito A. Evaluación de la efectividad de un programa de intervención cognitiva en memoria de trabajo [thesis]. Argentina: Universidad del Aconcagua; 2017

[31] Ortubia NL, Espósito A. Capacidad atencional en niños: programa de entrenamiento informatizado [thesis]. Argentina: Universidad del Aconcagua; 2015

[32] Canet Juric L, Stelzer F, Andrés ML, Vernucci S, Introzzi I, Burin DI. Evidence of validity of a computer task of verbal and viso-spatial work memory for children. Interamerican Journal of Psychology. 2018;**52**(1):112-128

[33] Richards M, Introzzi I, Zamora E, Vernucci S. Analysis of internal and external validity criteria for a computerized visual search task: A pilot study. Applied Neuropsychology: Child. 2017;**2**:110-119. DOI: 10.1080/21622965.2015.1083433

[34] Richards M, Vernucci S, Stelzer F, Introzzi I, Guardia-Olmos J. Exploratory data analysis of executive functions in children: A new assessment battery. Current Psychology. 2020;**39**:1610-1617. DOI: 10.1007/s12144-018-9860-4

[35] Syväoja HJ, Tammelin TH, Ahonen T, Räsänen P, Tolvanen A, Kankaanpää A, et al. Internal consistency and stability of the CANTAB neuropsychological test battery in children. Psychological Assessment. 2015;**27**(2):698-709. DOI: 10.1037/a0038485

[36] Fernández-Alcántara M, Albaladejo-Blázquez N, Fernández-Ávalos MI, Sánchez-San Segundo M, Cruz-Quintana F, Pérez-Martínez V, et al. Validity of the computerized battery for neuropsychological evaluation of children (BENCI) in Spanish children: Preliminary results. European Journal of Investigation in Health, Psychology and Education. 2022;**12**:893-903. DOI: 10.3390/ejihpe12080065

[37] Figueroa-Quiñones J, Moncada Oliva R, Coronado Zapata CA, Bazo-Alvarez JC. Test adaptativos informatizados, pruebas computarizadas y pruebas en aplicaciones móviles: comparación de su disponibilidad actual en Latinoamérica, Estados Unidos y Canadá. Aloma-Revista de Psicologia, Ciències de l'Eduació i de l'Esport. 2020;**38**(2):121-136